You Put *What* in the Punch? Annotated photos by Eugene J. Martin

Suzanne Fredericq

ISBN: 978-0-578-03043-2

Foreword

Contemporary visual artist Eugene James Martin takes a stroll on the sunny side of the street, clicks, clicks, clicks, and has fun, fun, fun.

Suzanne Fredericq,
Lafayette, Louisiana, June 24, 2009

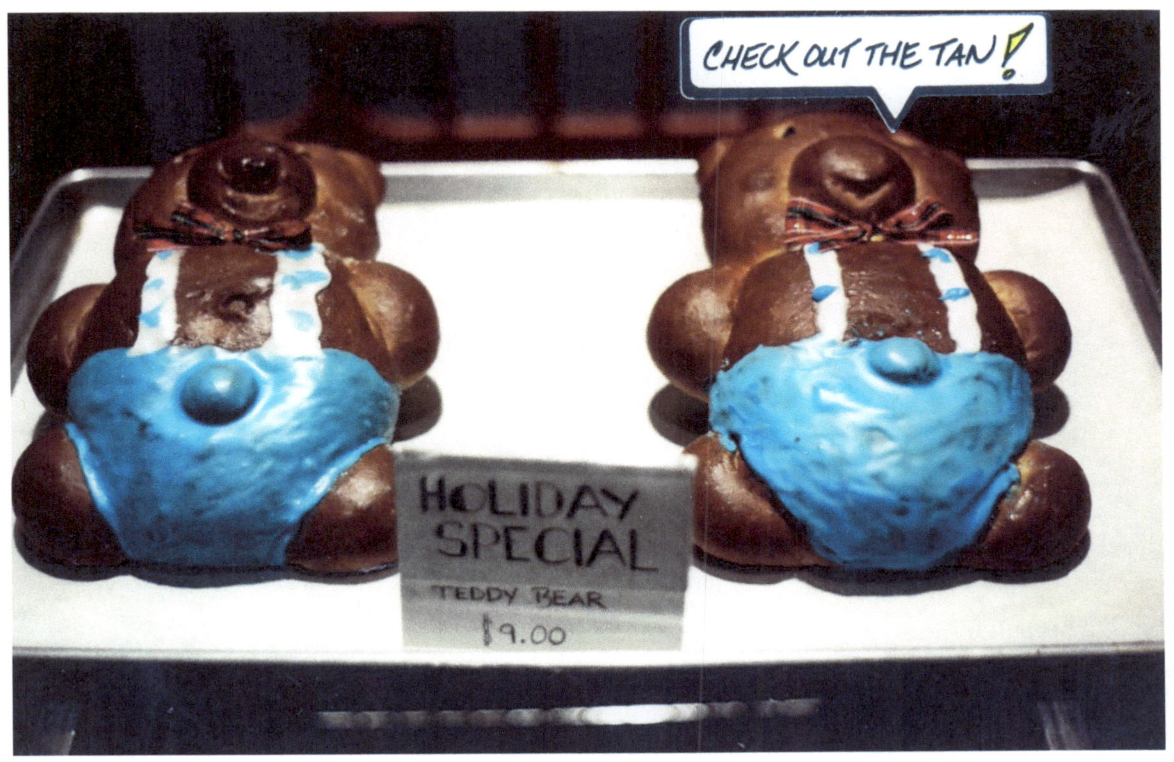
CHECK OUT THE TAN!
HOLIDAY SPECIAL
TEDDY BEAR
$9.00

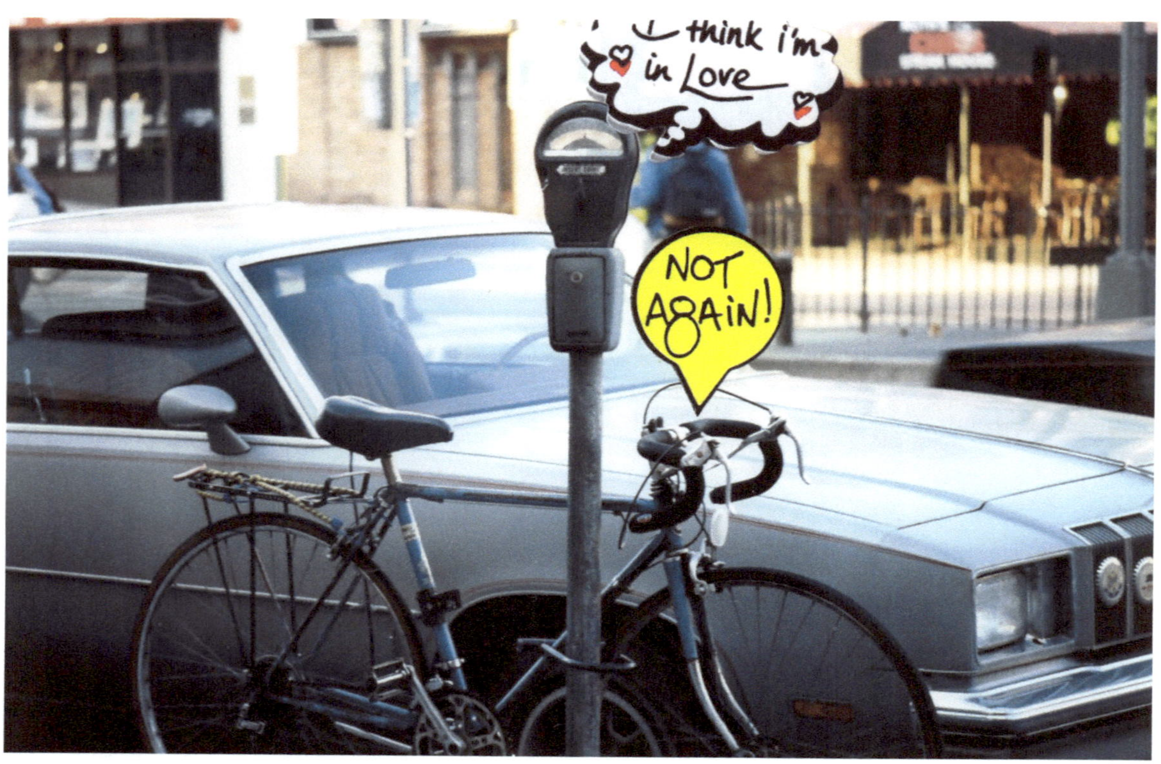
think i'm
in Love
NOT AGAIN!

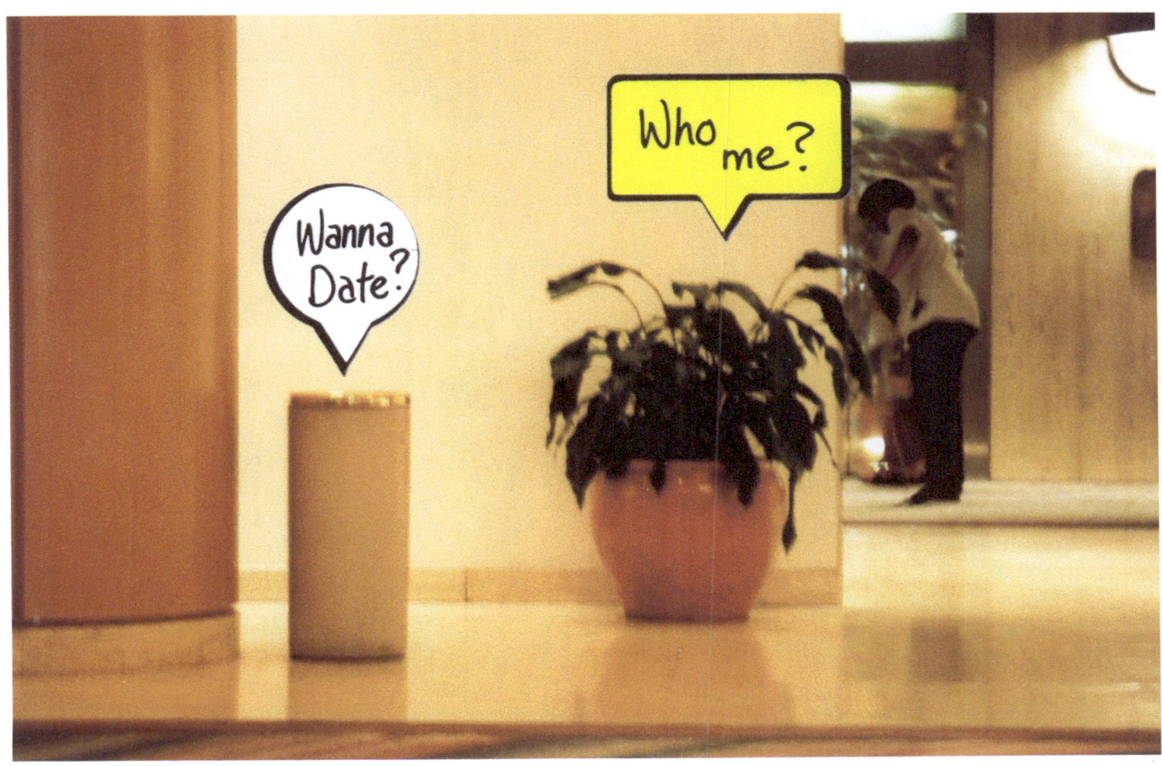
Wanna Date?
Who me?

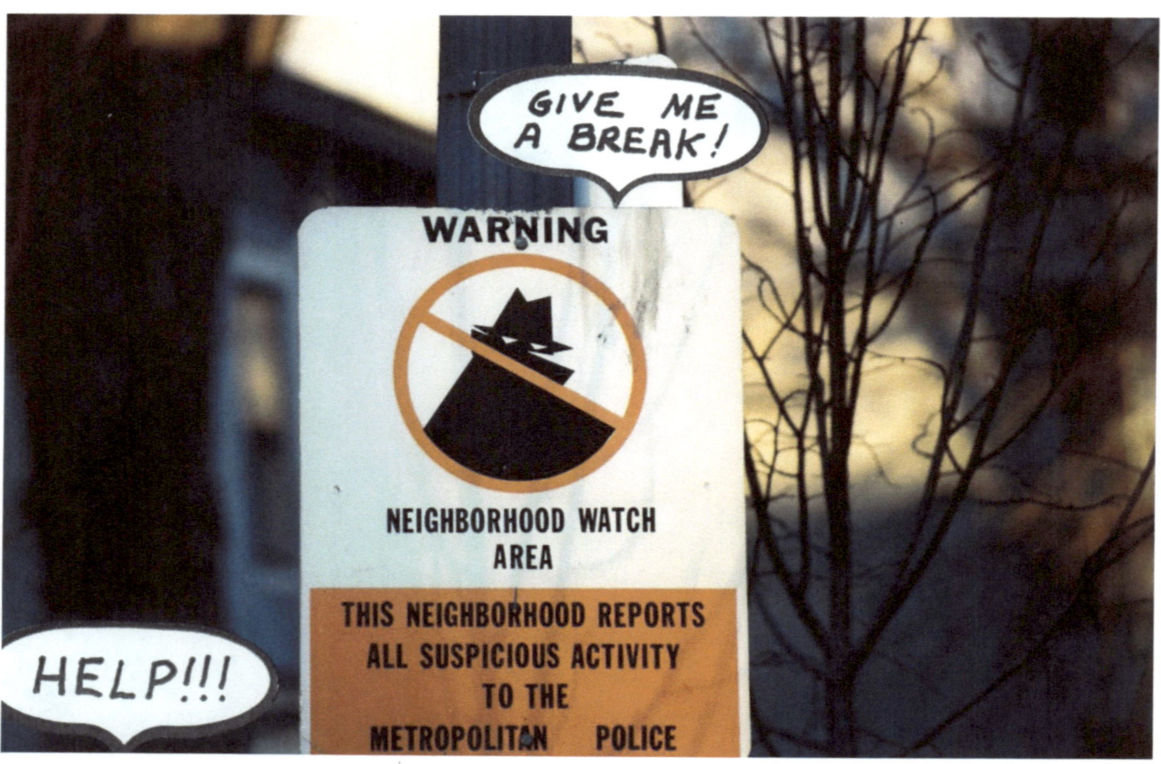
GIVE ME
A BREAK!
WARNING
NEIGHBORHOOD WATCH
AREA
THIS NEIGHBORHOOD REPORTS
ALL SUSPICIOUS ACTIVITY
TO THE
METROPOLITAN POLICE
HELP!!!

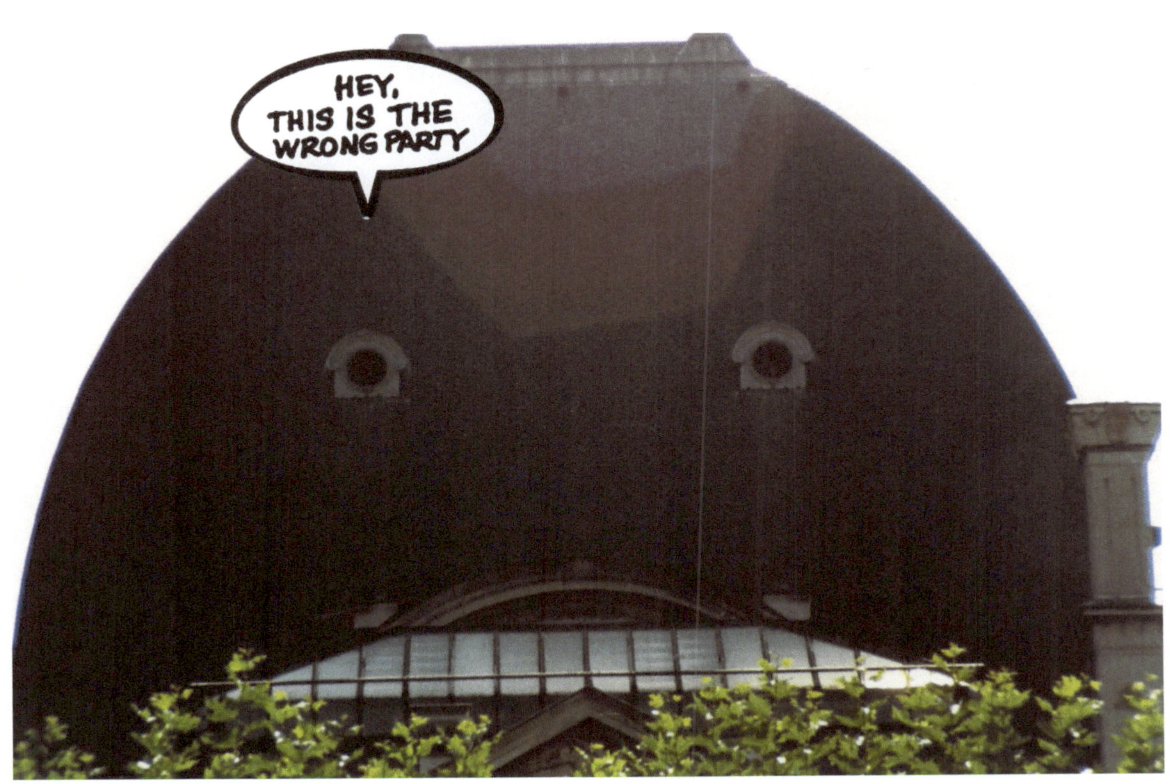
HEY,
THIS IS THE
WRONG PARTY

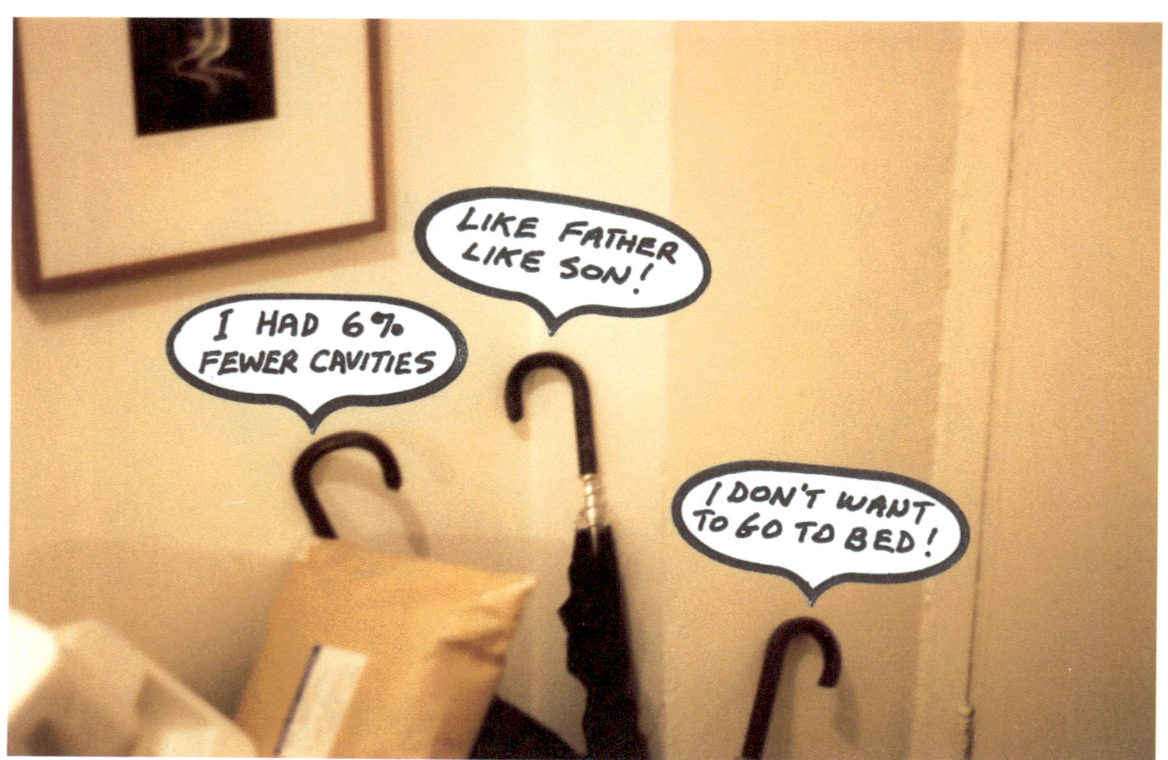
I HAD 6%
FEWER CAVITIES
LIKE FATHER
LIKE SON!
I DON'T WANT
TO GO TO BED!

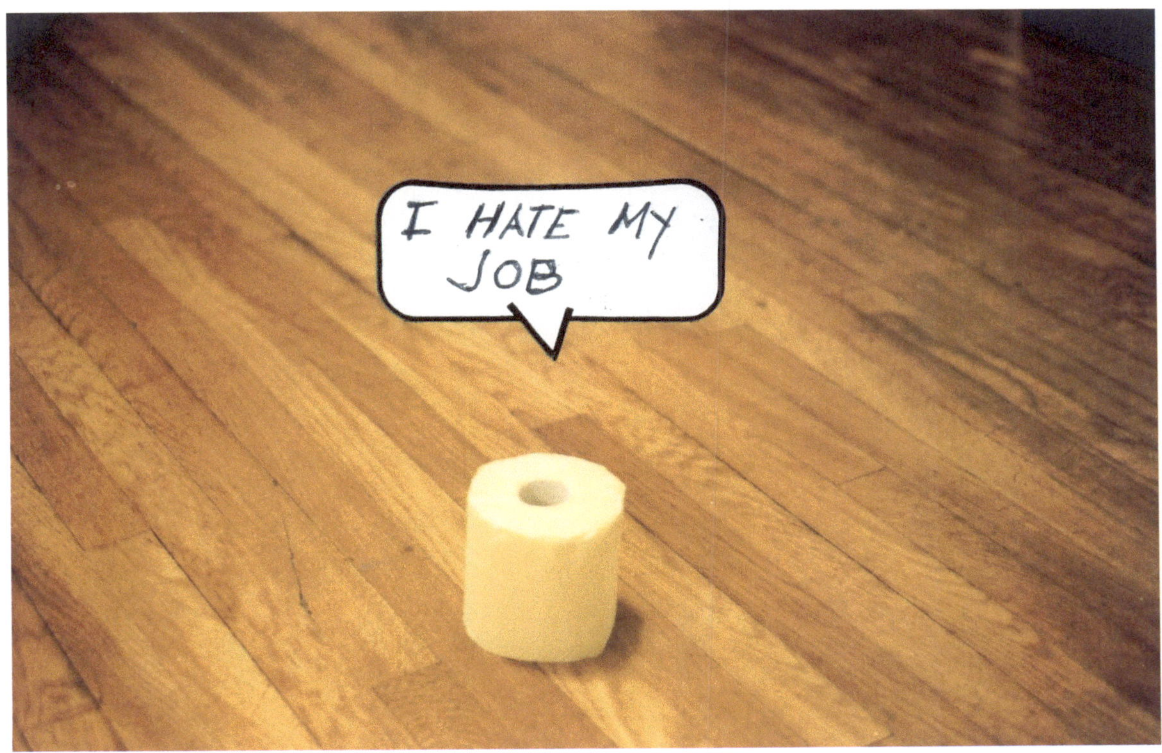
I HATE MY JOB

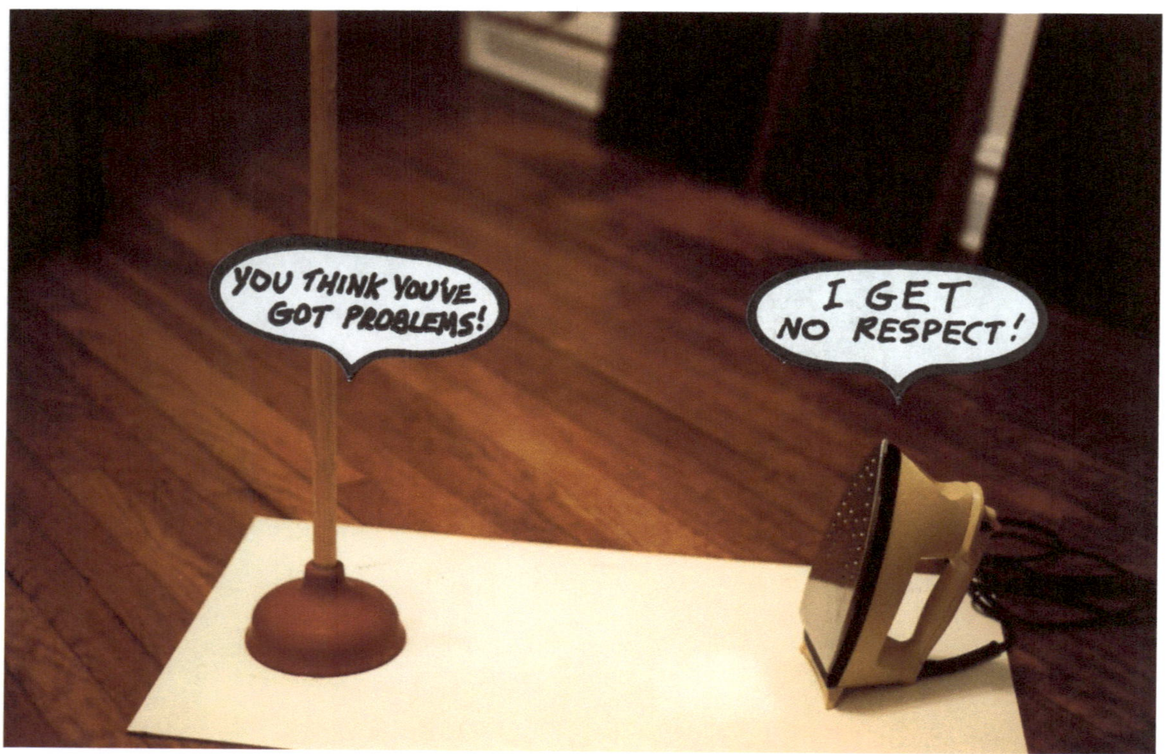
YOU THINK YOU'VE GOT PROBLEMS!
I GET NO RESPECT!

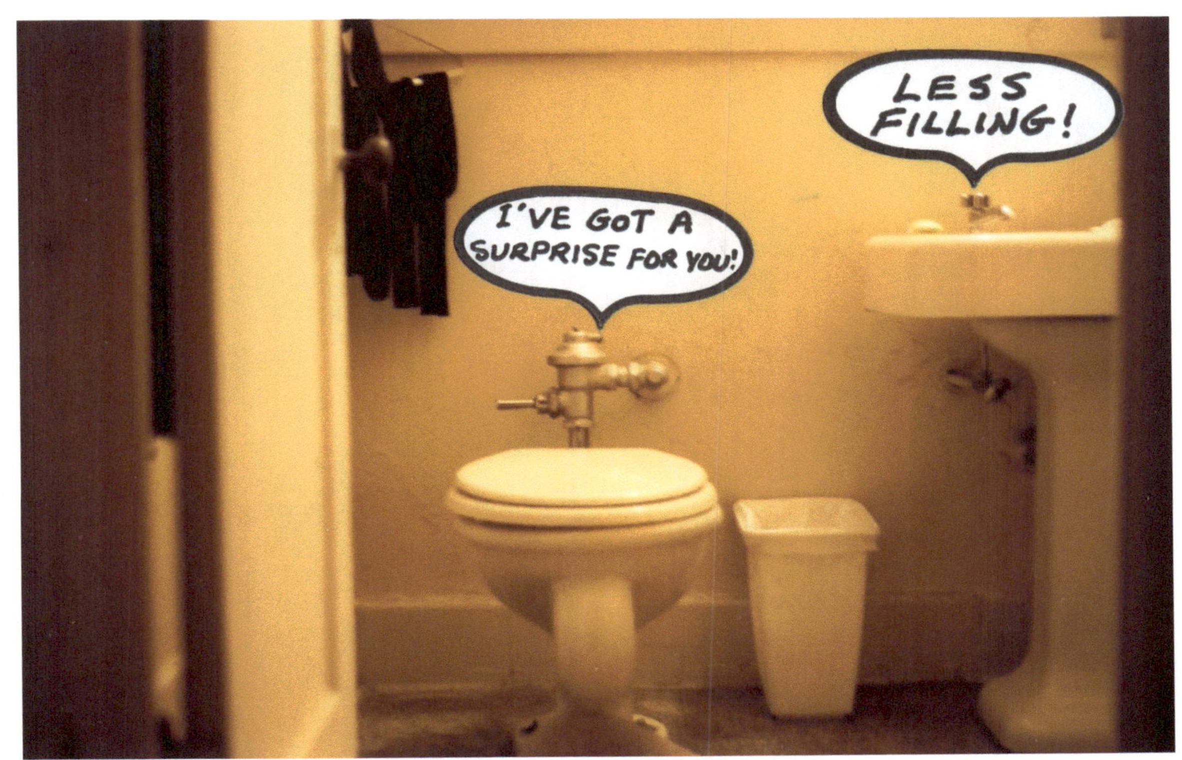
I'VE GOT A SURPRISE FOR YOU!
LESS FILLING!

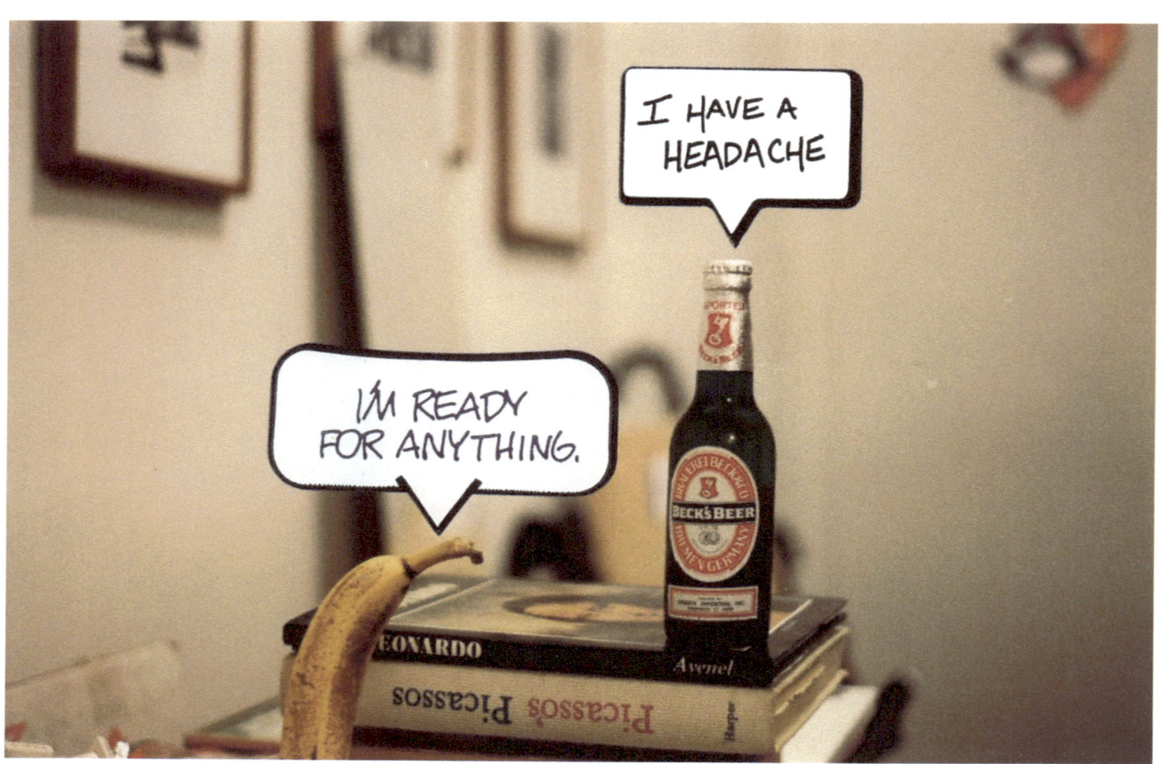
I'M READY
FOR ANYTHING.
I HAVE A
HEADACHE
BECK'S BEER
Avenel

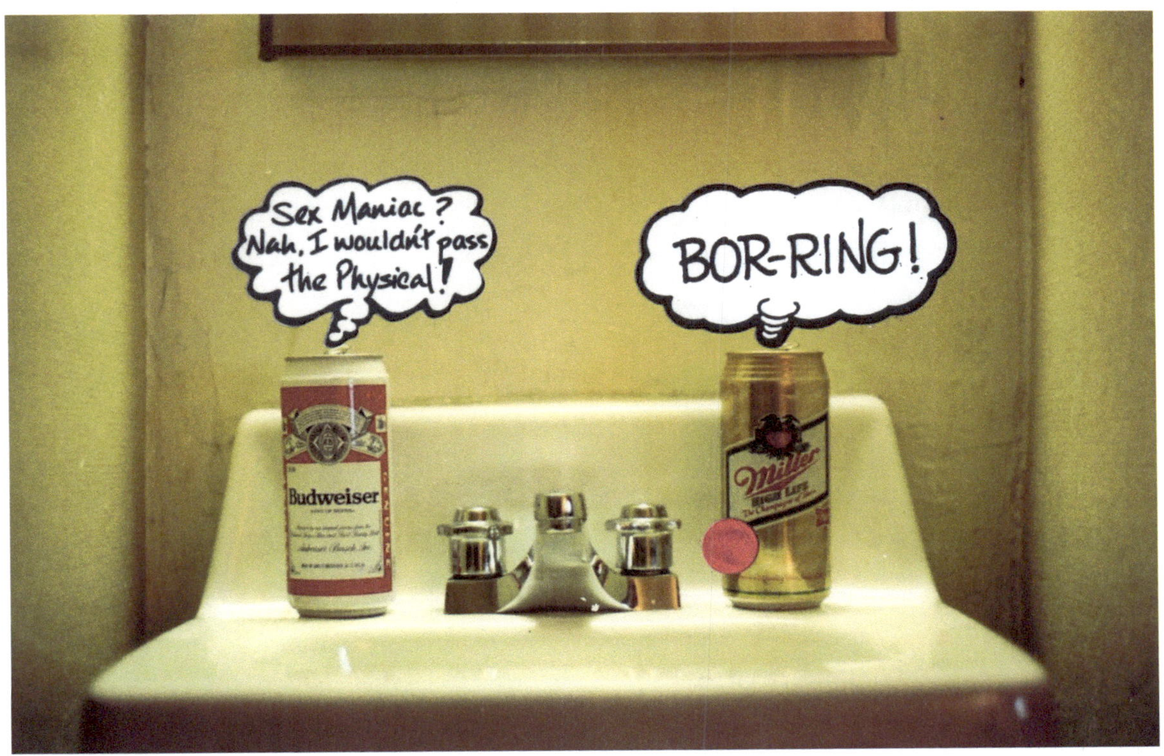
Sex Maniac? Nah, I wouldn't pass the Physical!
BOR-RING!
Budweiser
Miller
HIGH LIFE

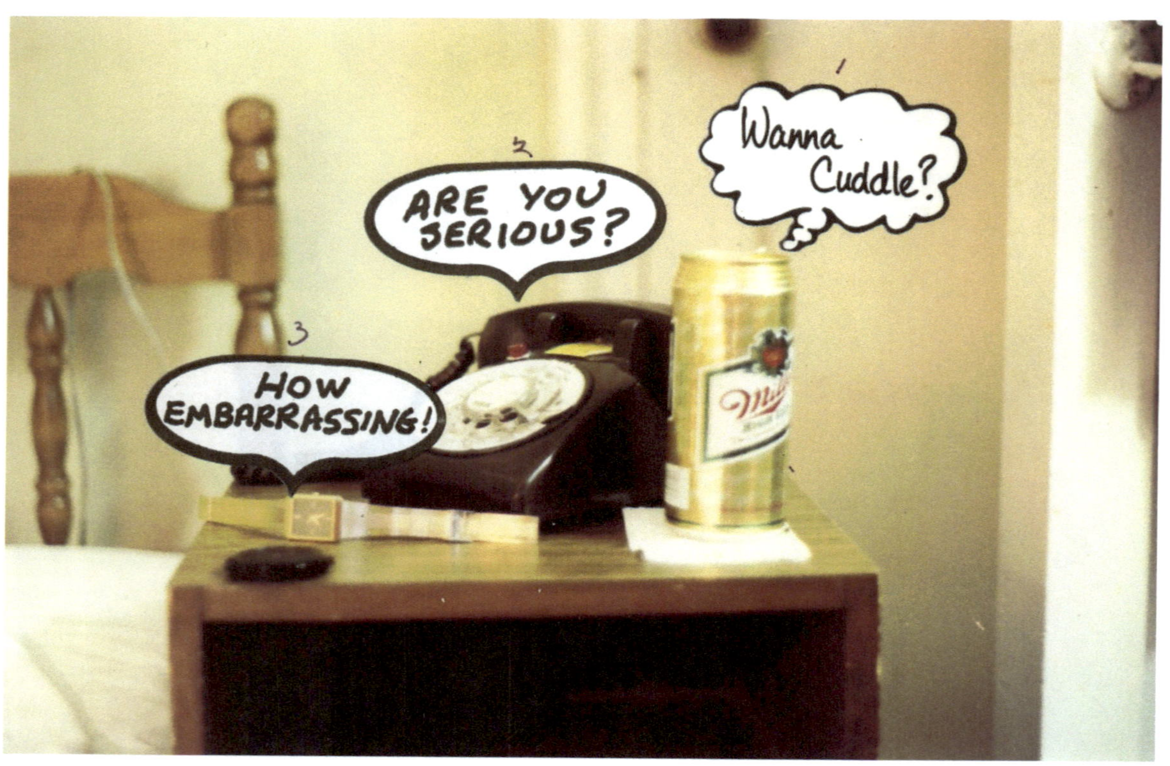
Wanna Cuddle?
ARE YOU SERIOUS?
HOW EMBARRASSING!

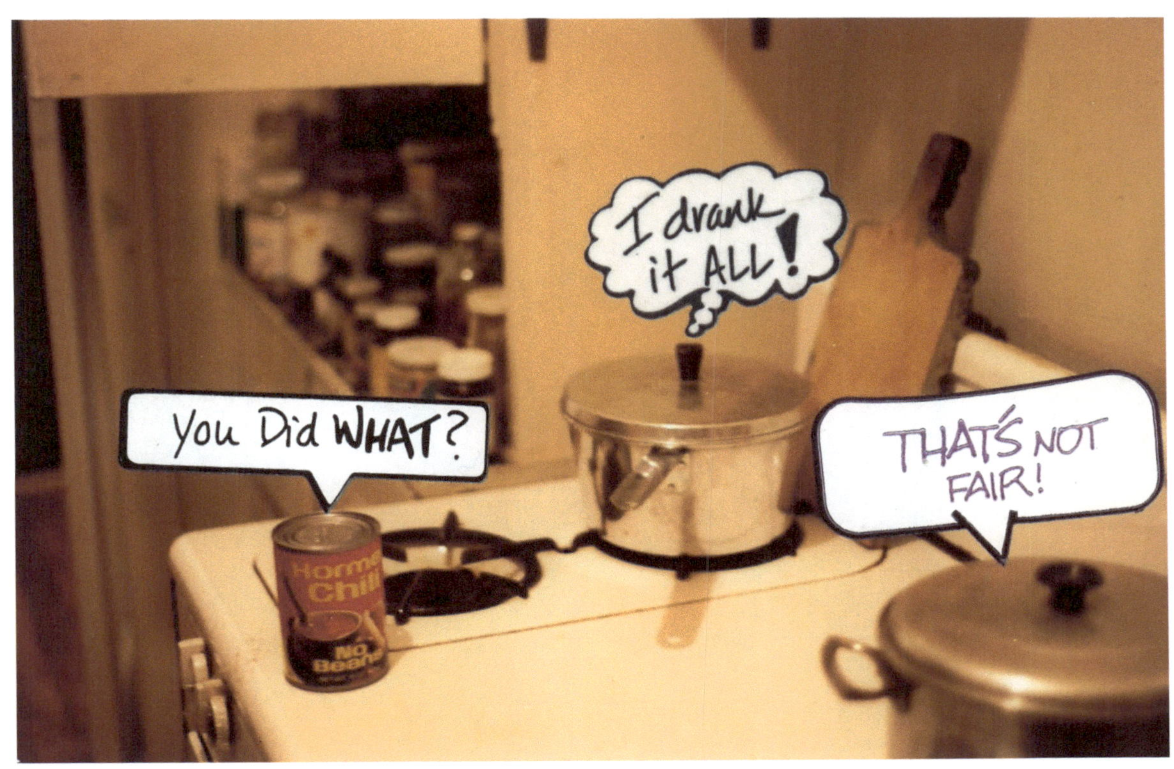
You Did WHAT?
I drank it ALL!
THAT'S NOT FAIR!

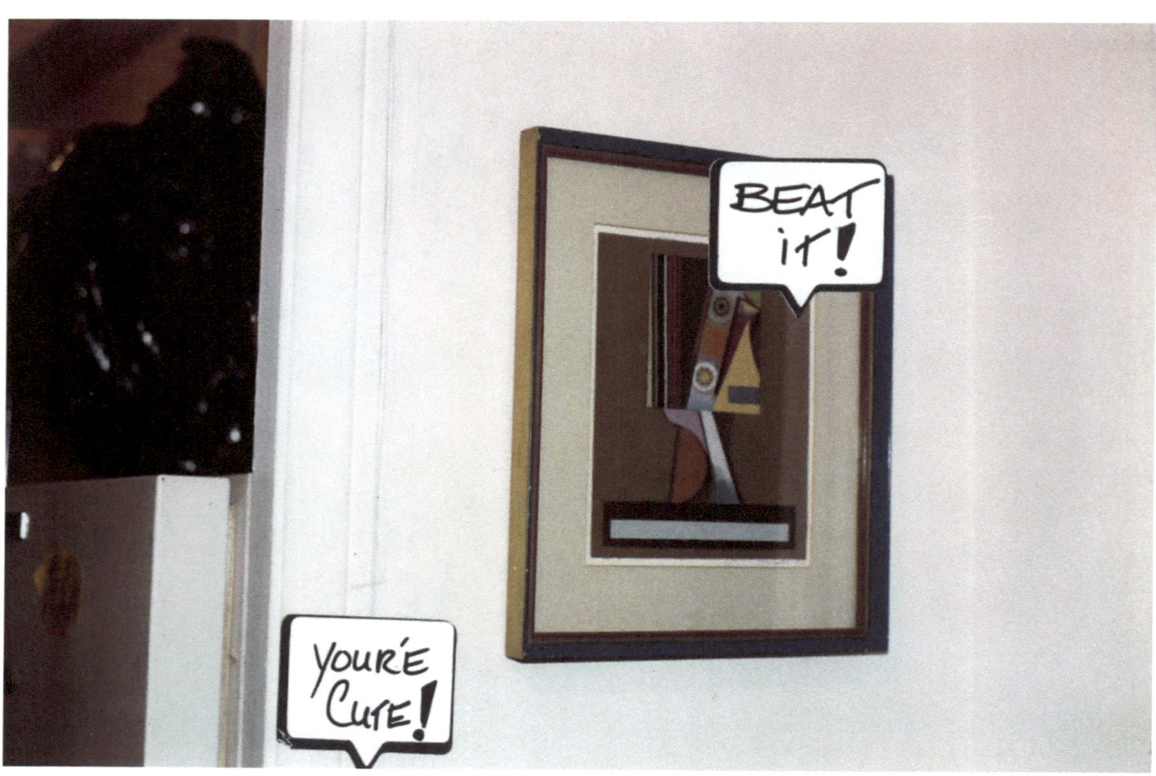
BEAT it!
YOU'RE CUTE!

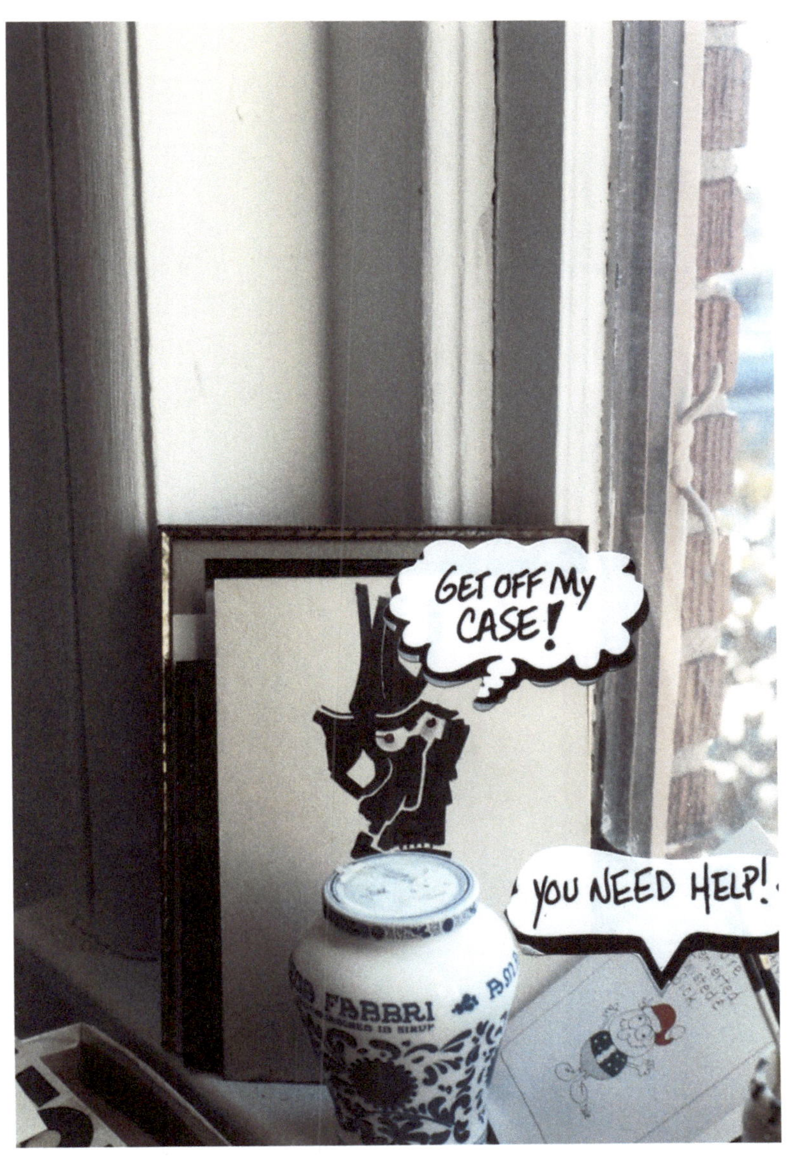
GET OFF MY CASE!
YOU NEED HELP!
FABBRI

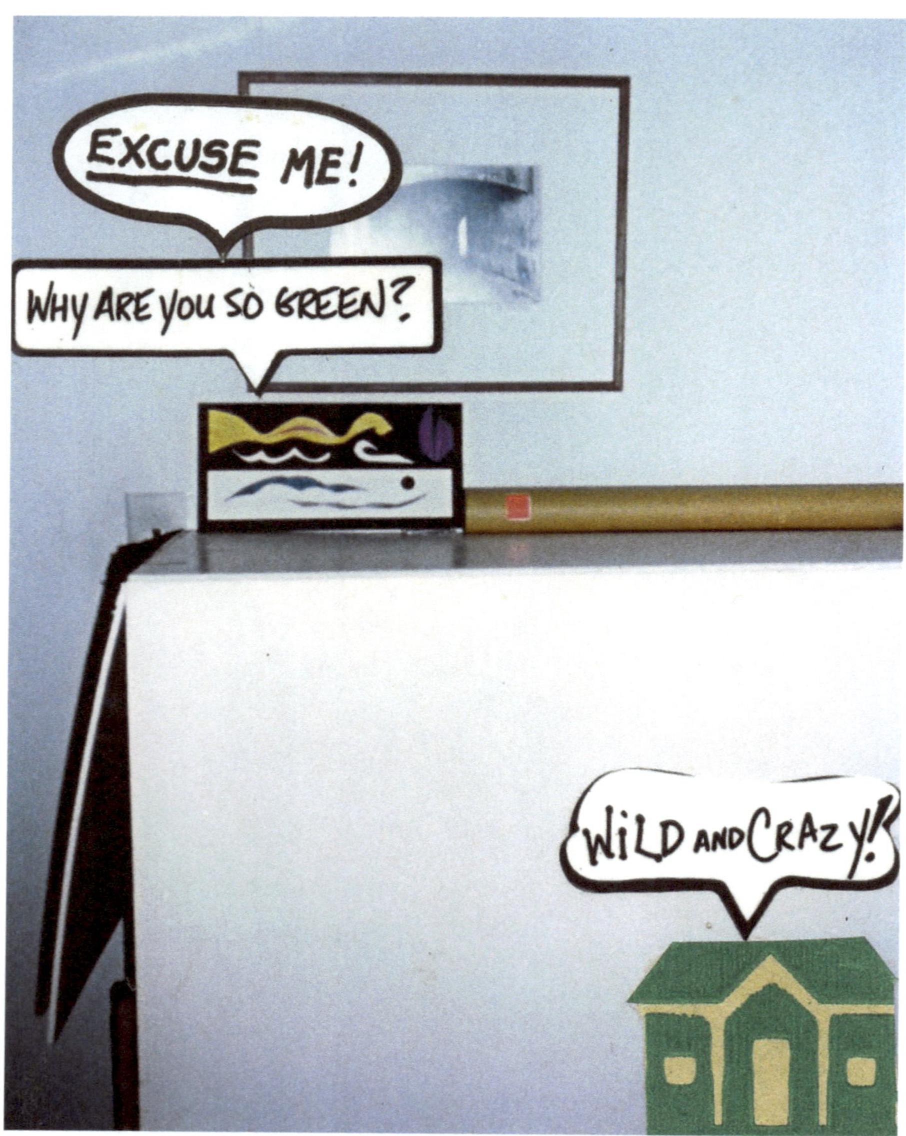
EXCUSE ME!
WHY ARE YOU SO GREEN?
WILD AND CRAZY!

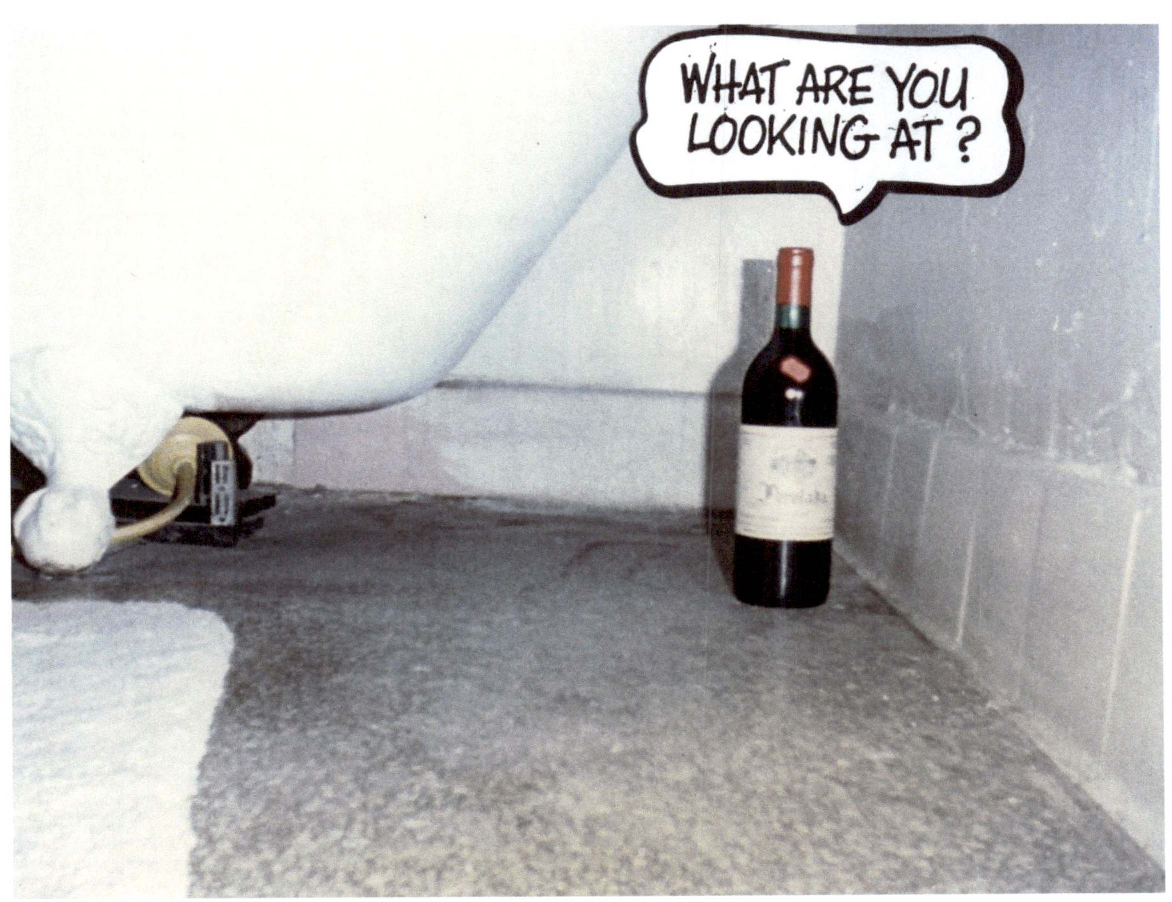
WHAT ARE YOU
LOOKING AT ?

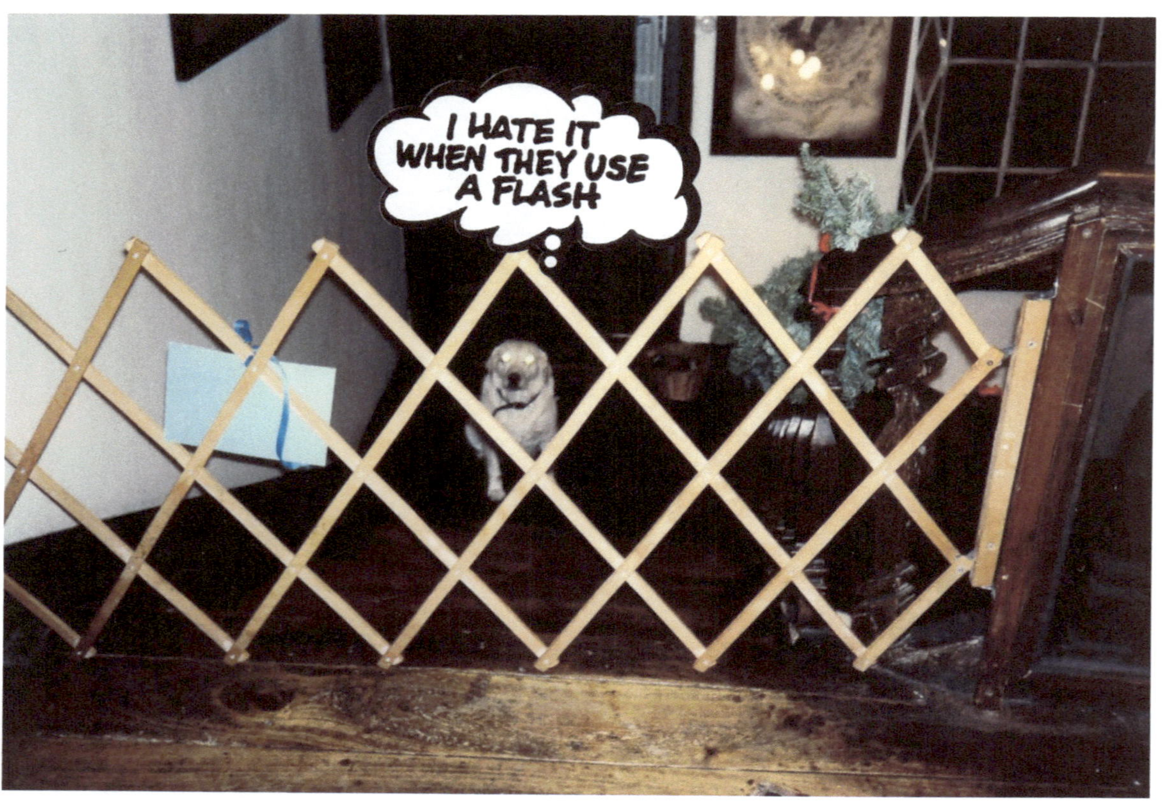
I HATE IT
WHEN THEY USE
A FLASH

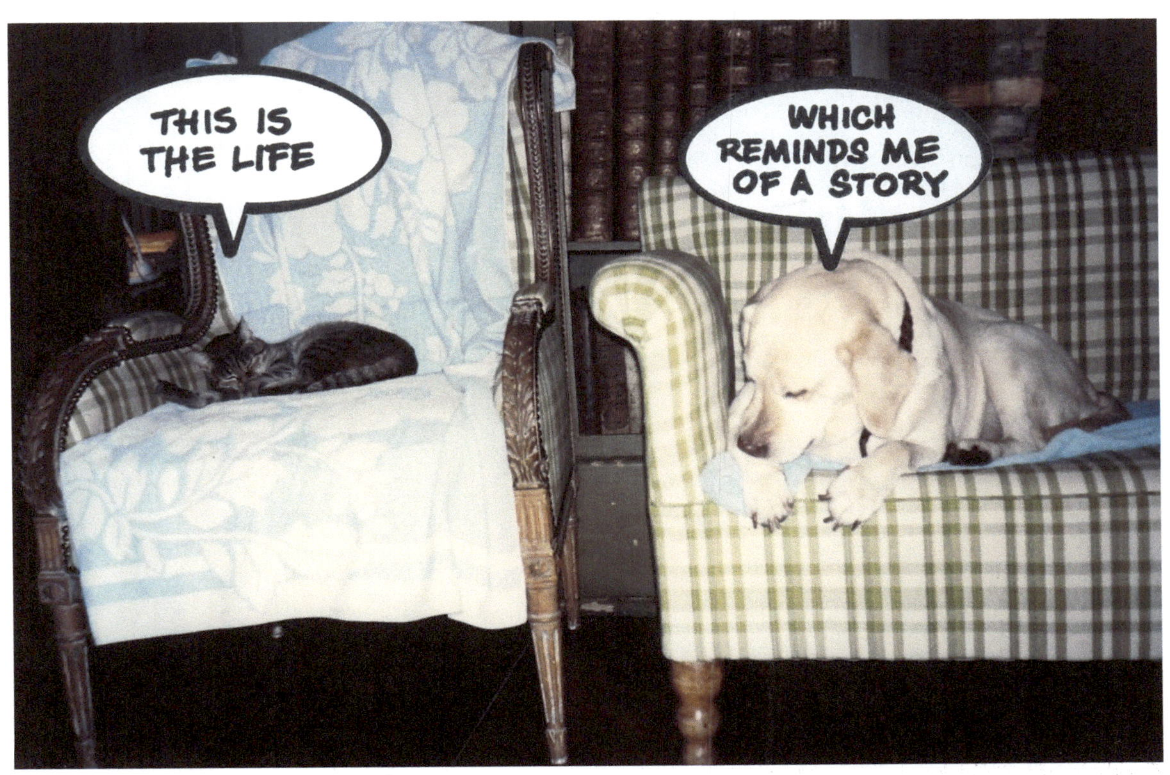
THIS IS THE LIFE
WHICH REMINDS ME OF A STORY

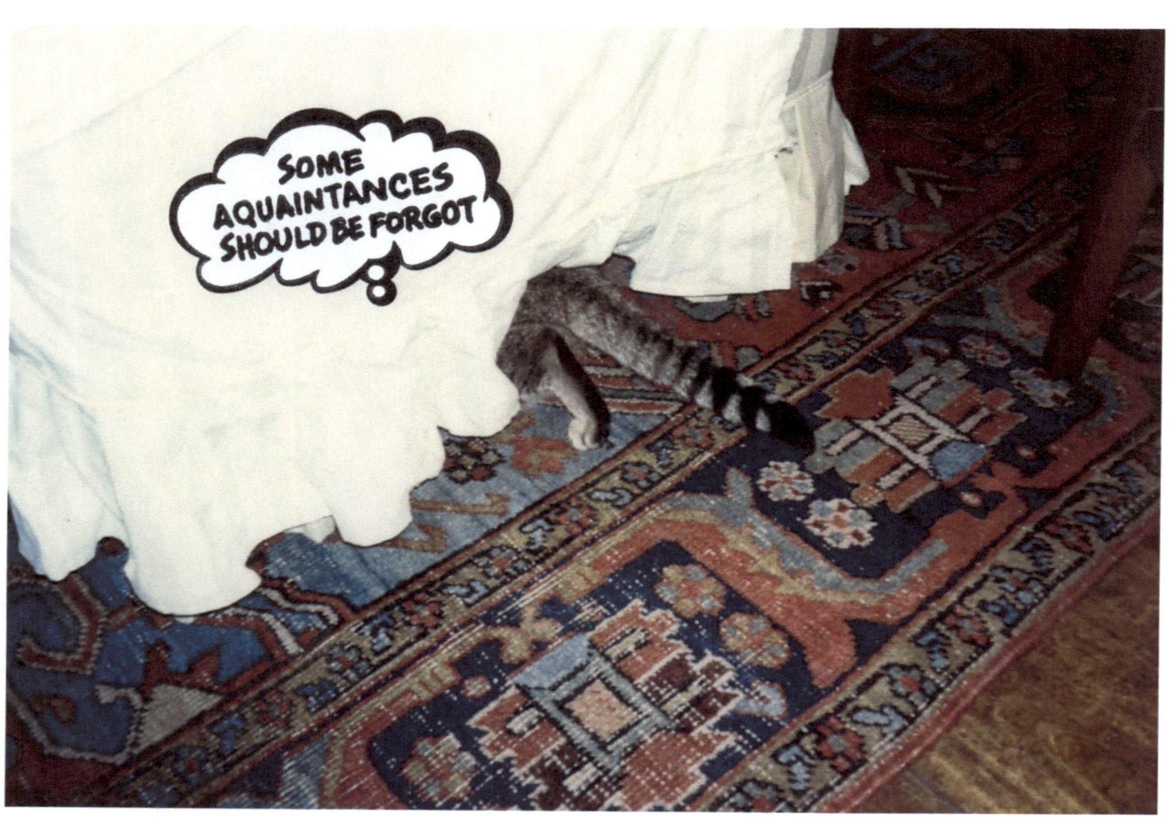
SOME
AQUAINTANCES
SHOULD BE FORGOT

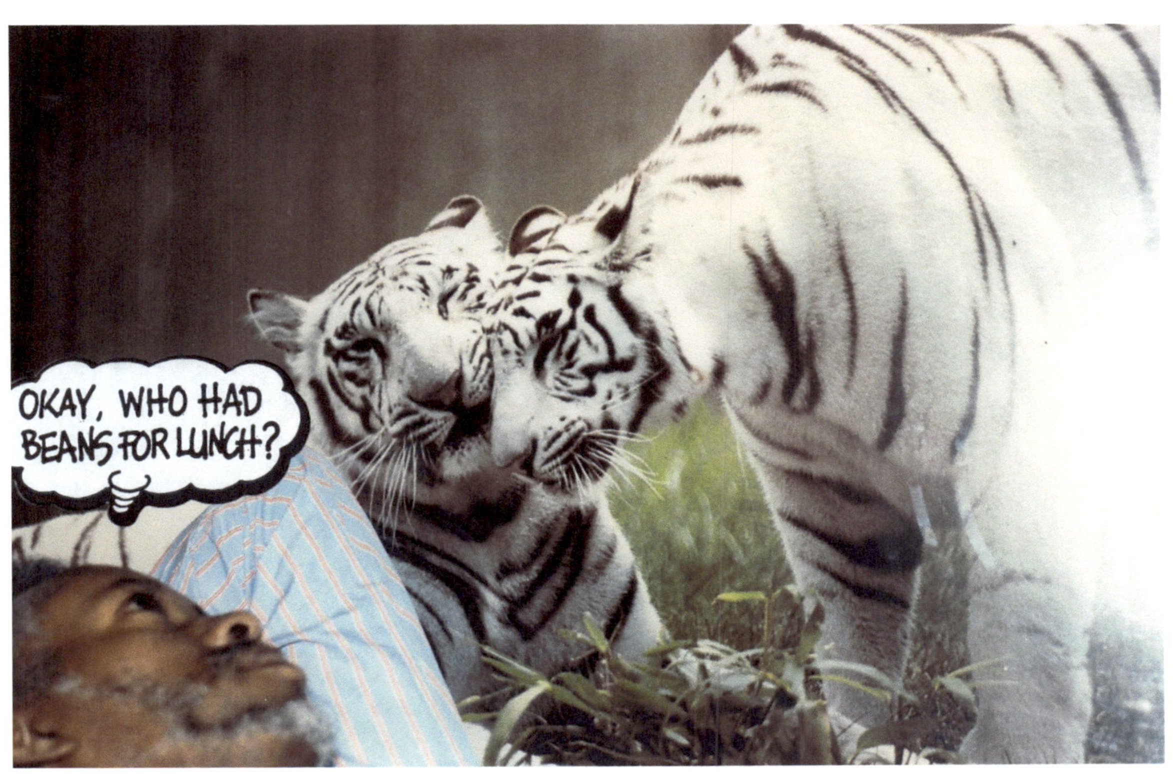
OKAY, WHO HAD BEANS FOR LUNCH?

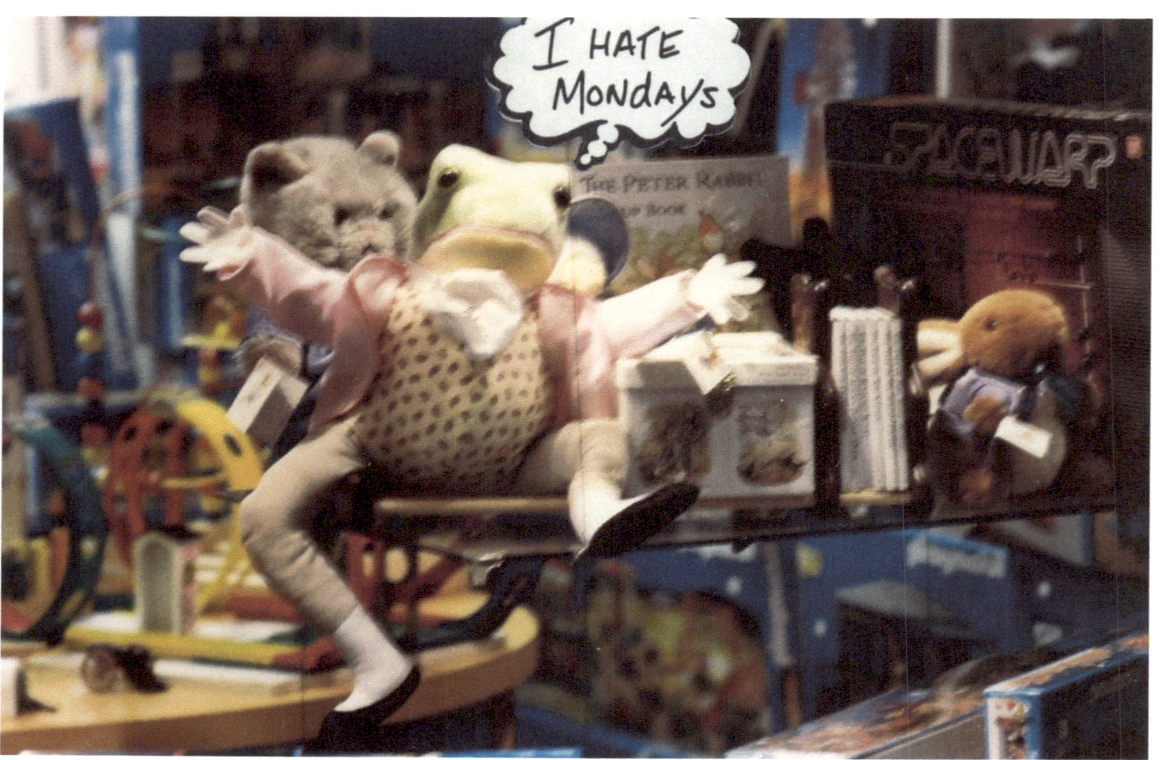
I HATE
MONDAYS
SPACEWARP

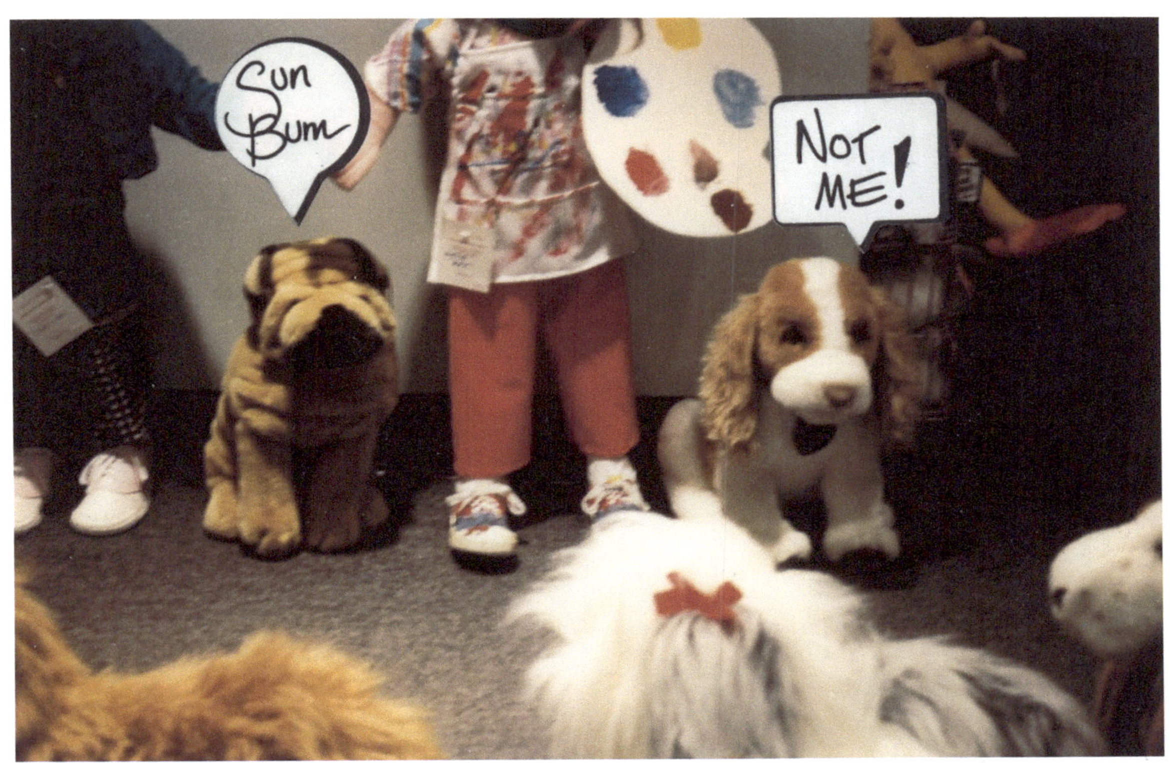
Sun Bum
NOT ME!

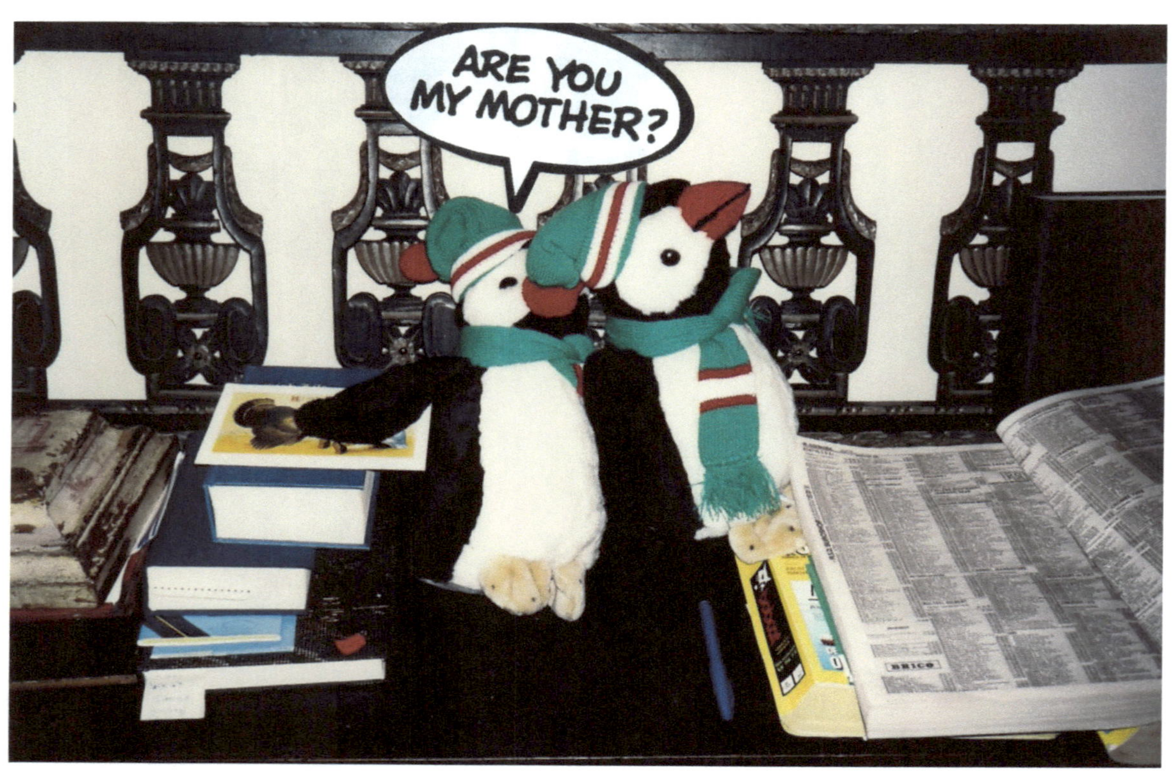
ARE YOU MY MOTHER?

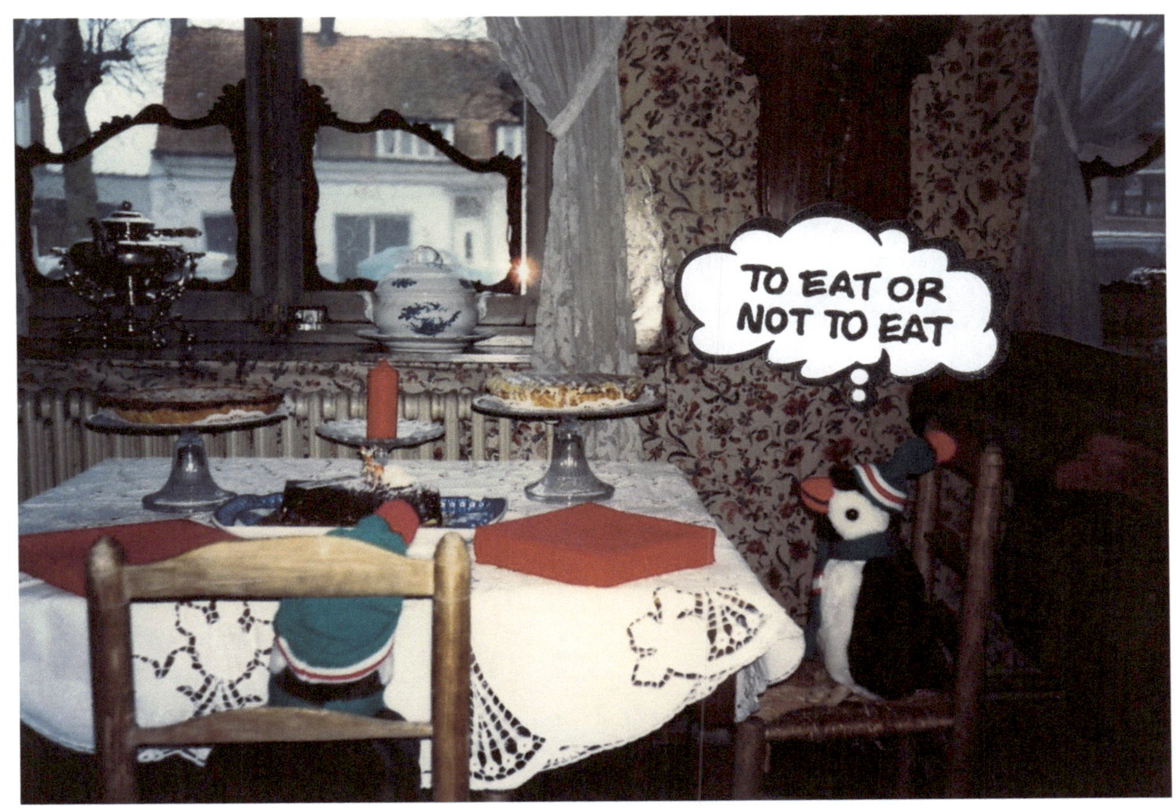
TO EAT OR
NOT TO EAT

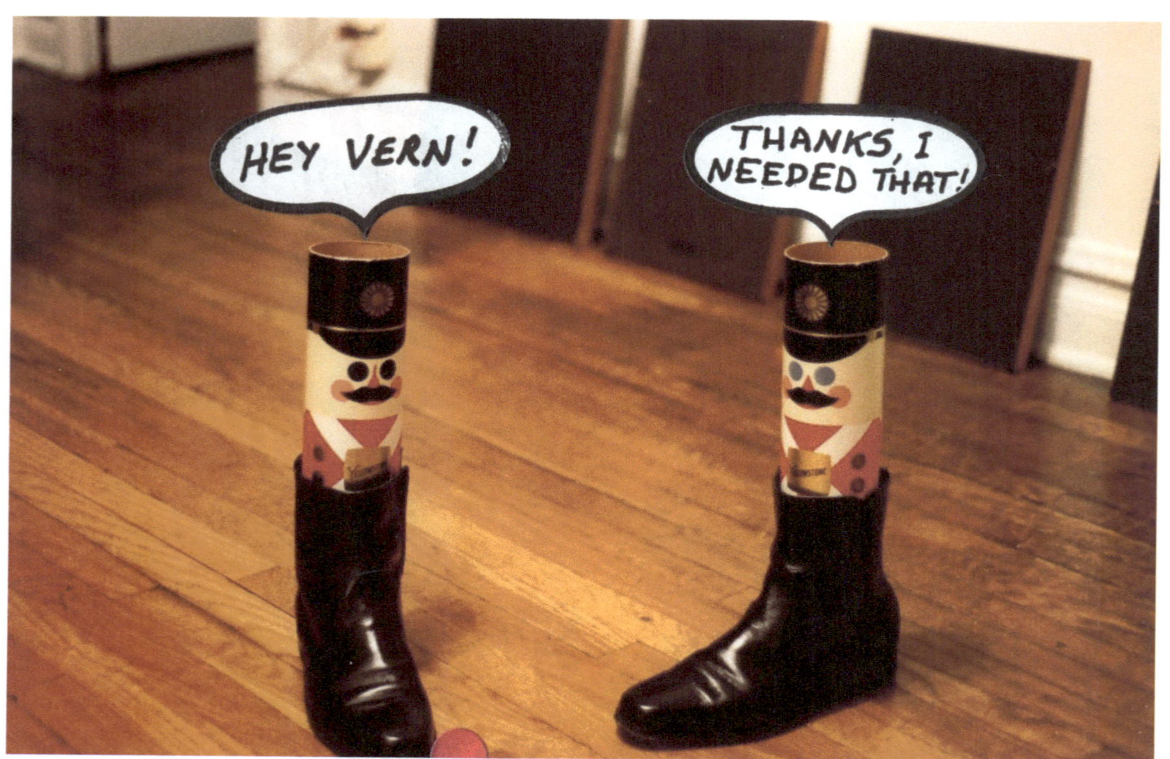
HEY VERN!
THANKS, I NEEDED THAT!

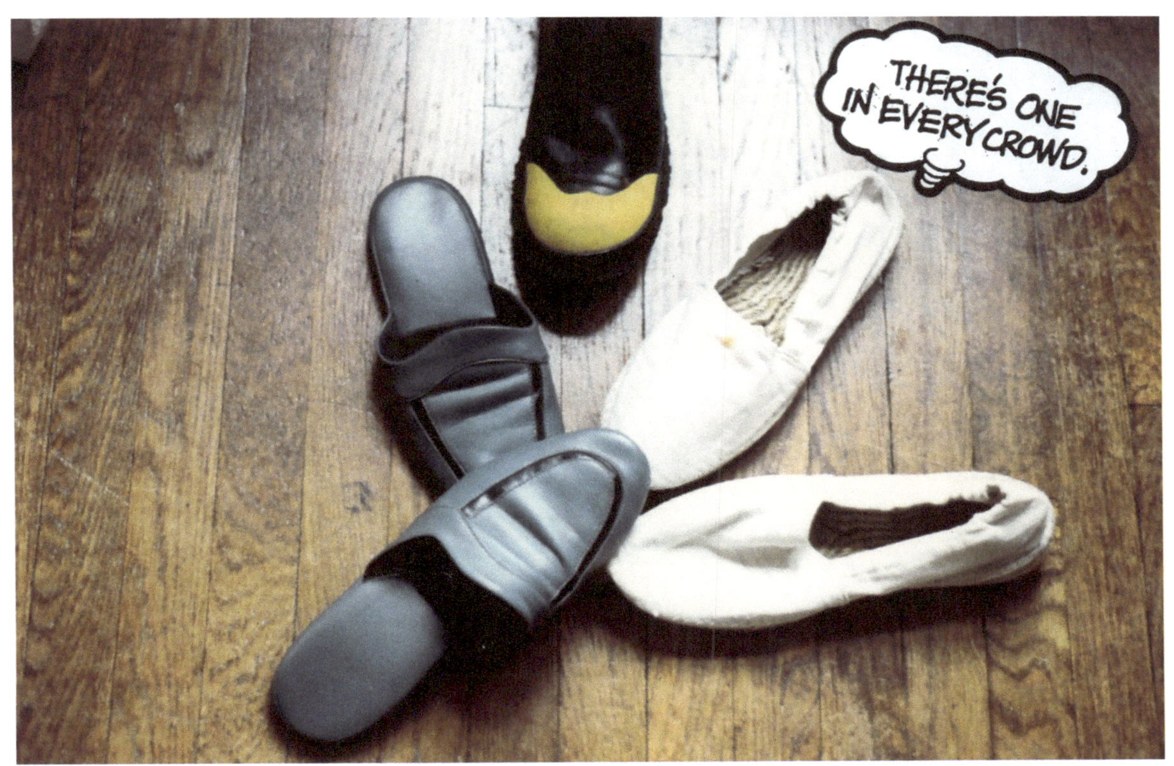
THERE'S ONE
IN EVERY CROWD.

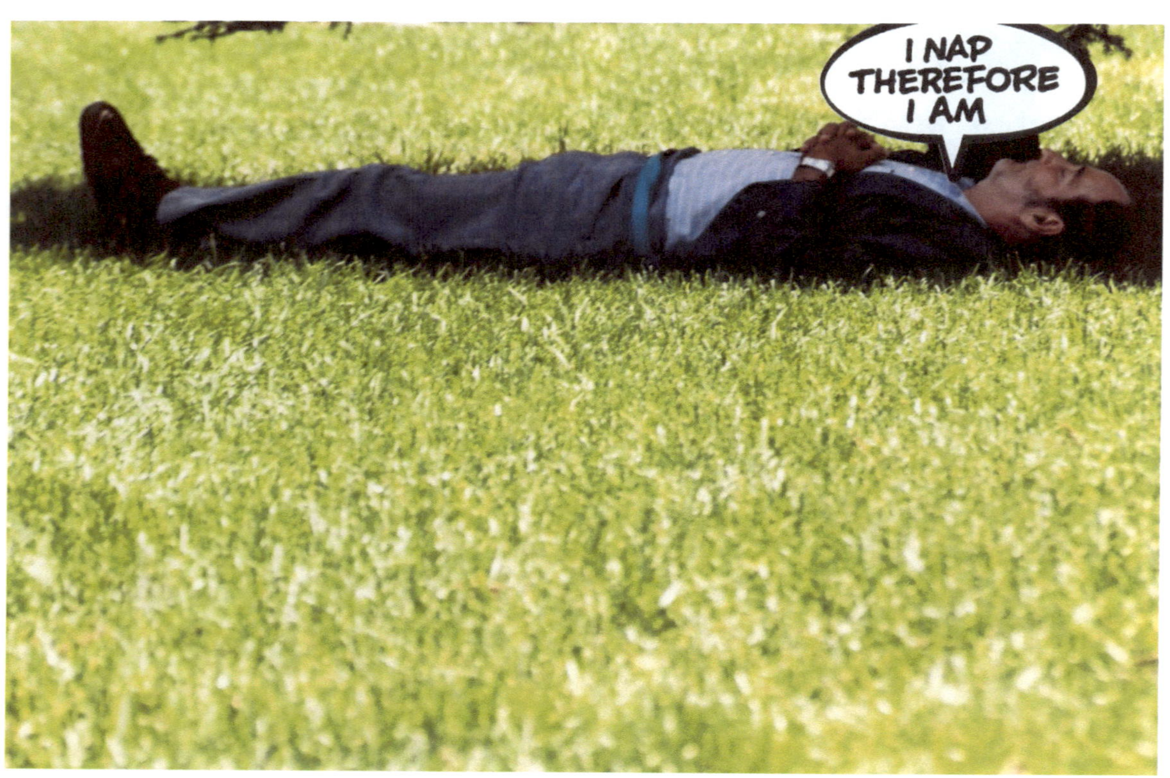
I NAP
THEREFORE
I AM

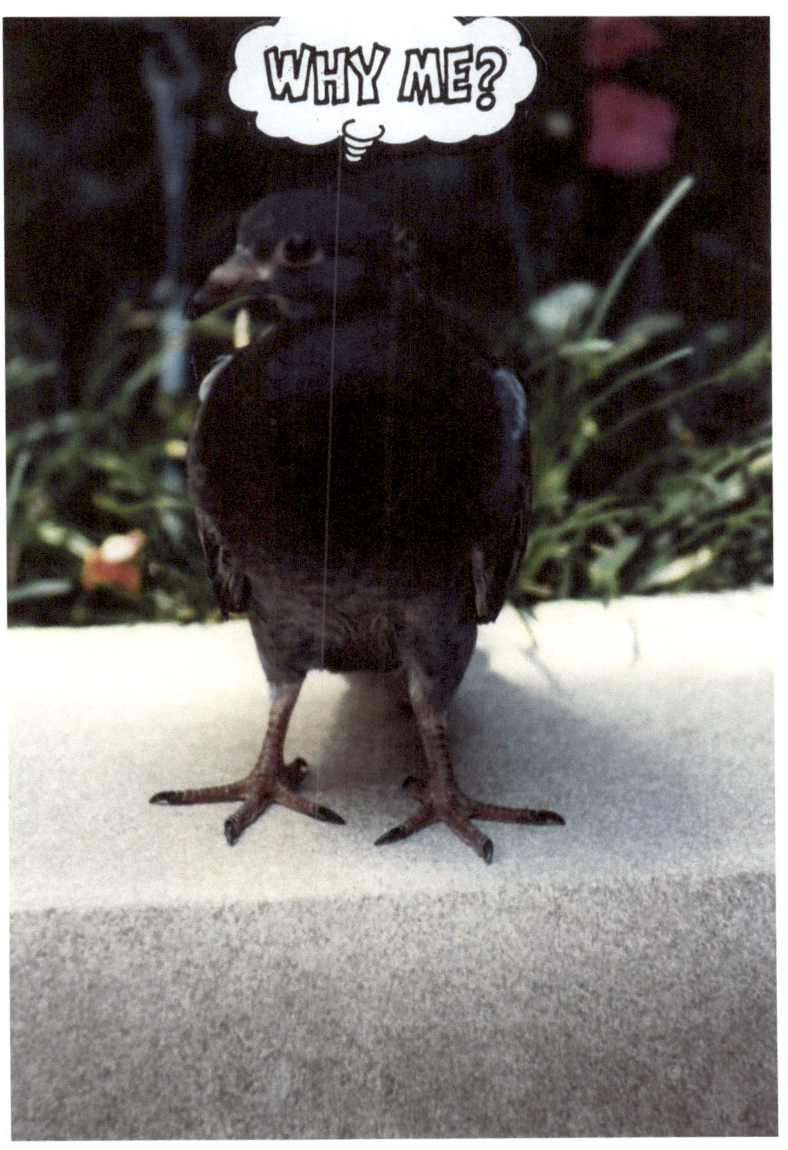
WHY ME?

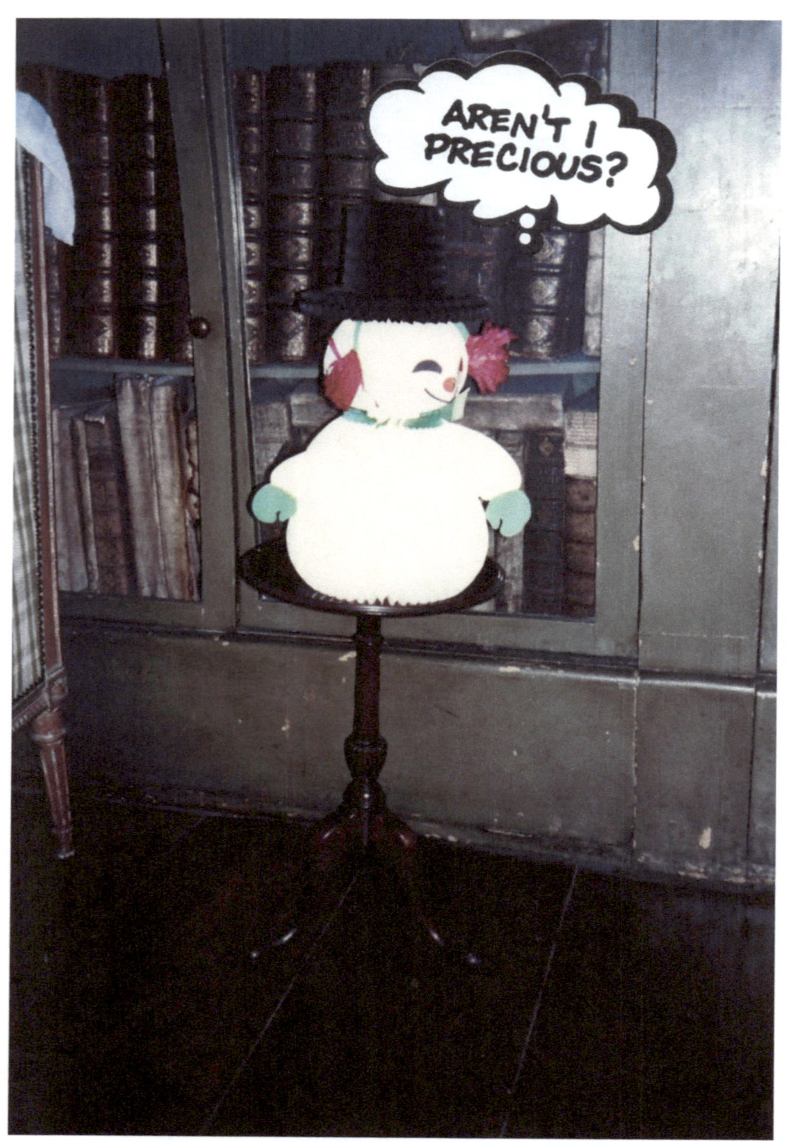
AREN'T I PRECIOUS?

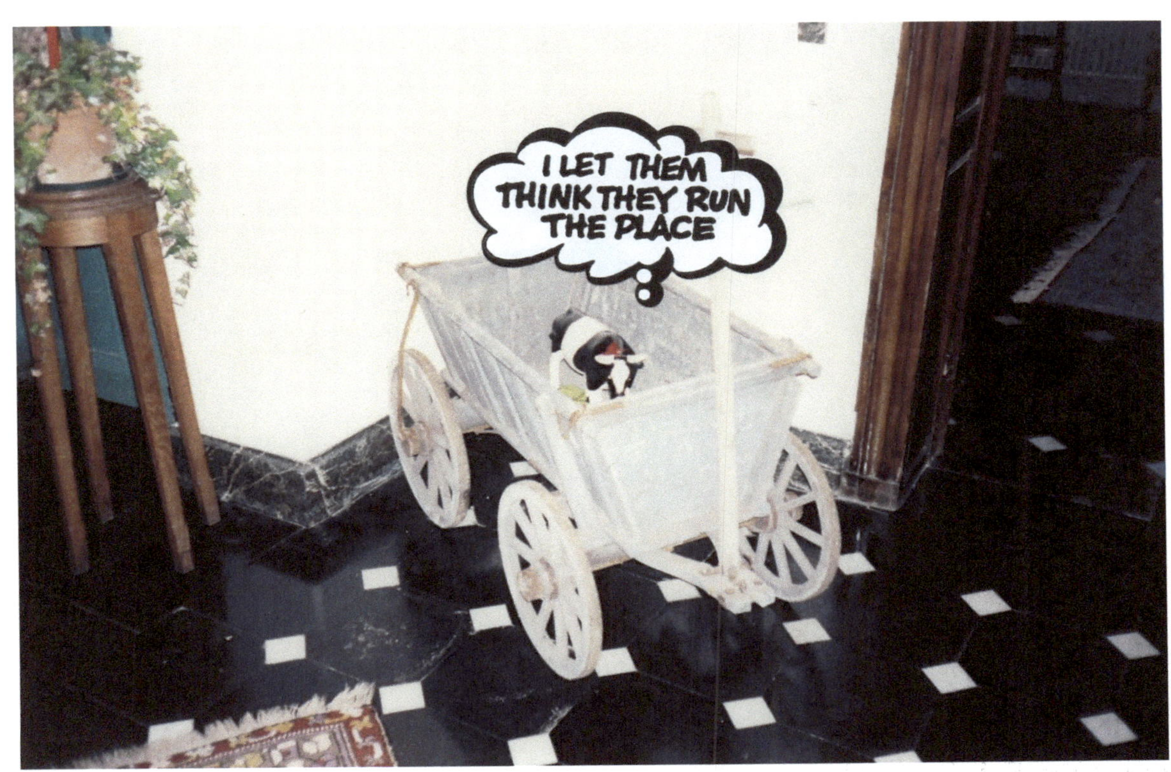
I LET THEM
THINK THEY RUN
THE PLACE

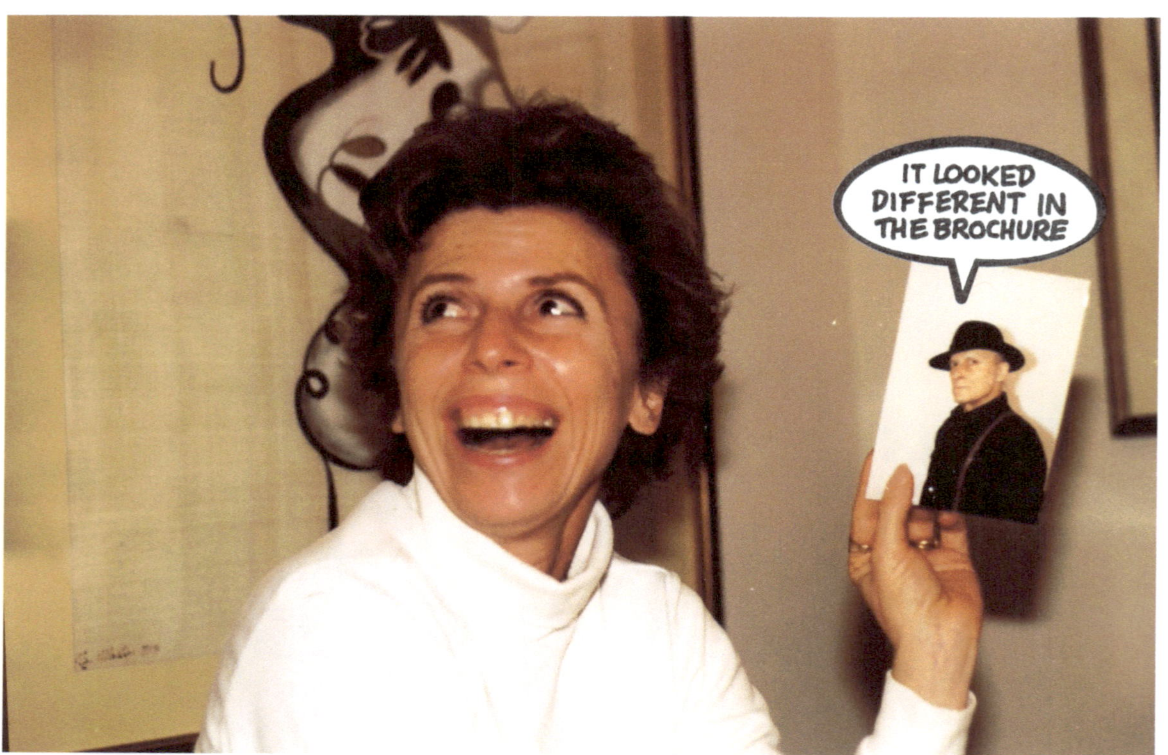
IT LOOKED DIFFERENT IN THE BROCHURE

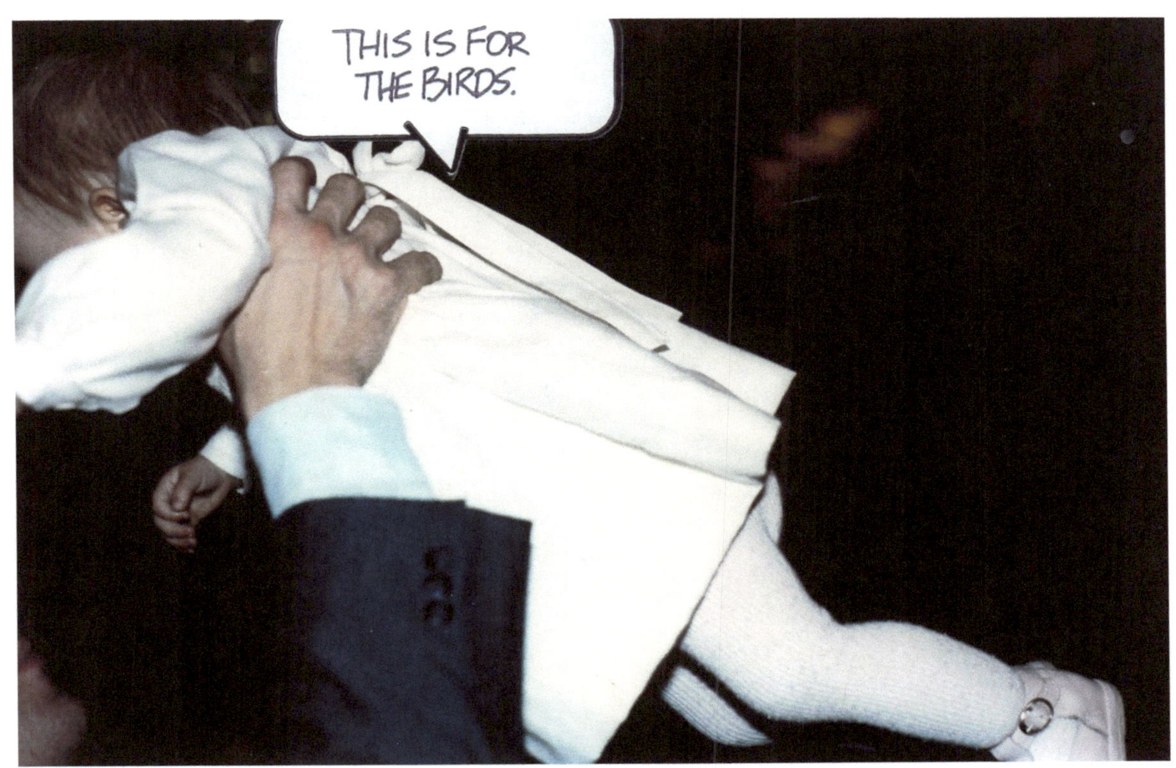
THIS IS FOR THE BIRDS.

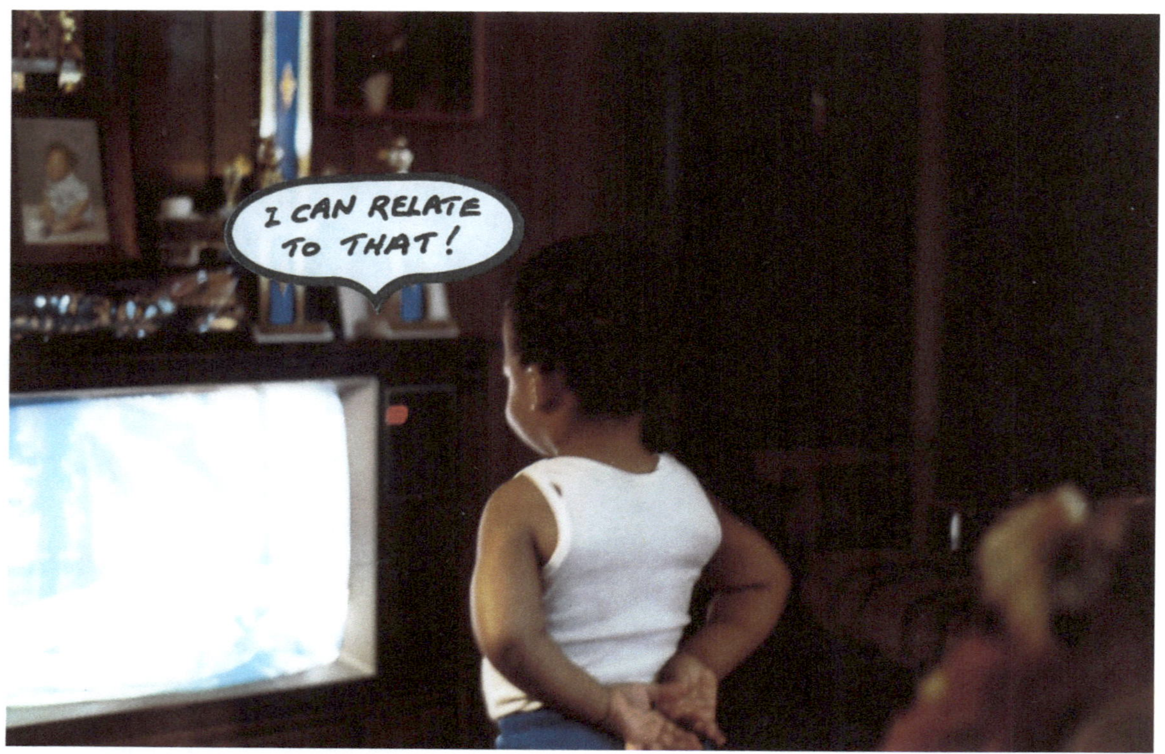
I CAN RELATE TO THAT!

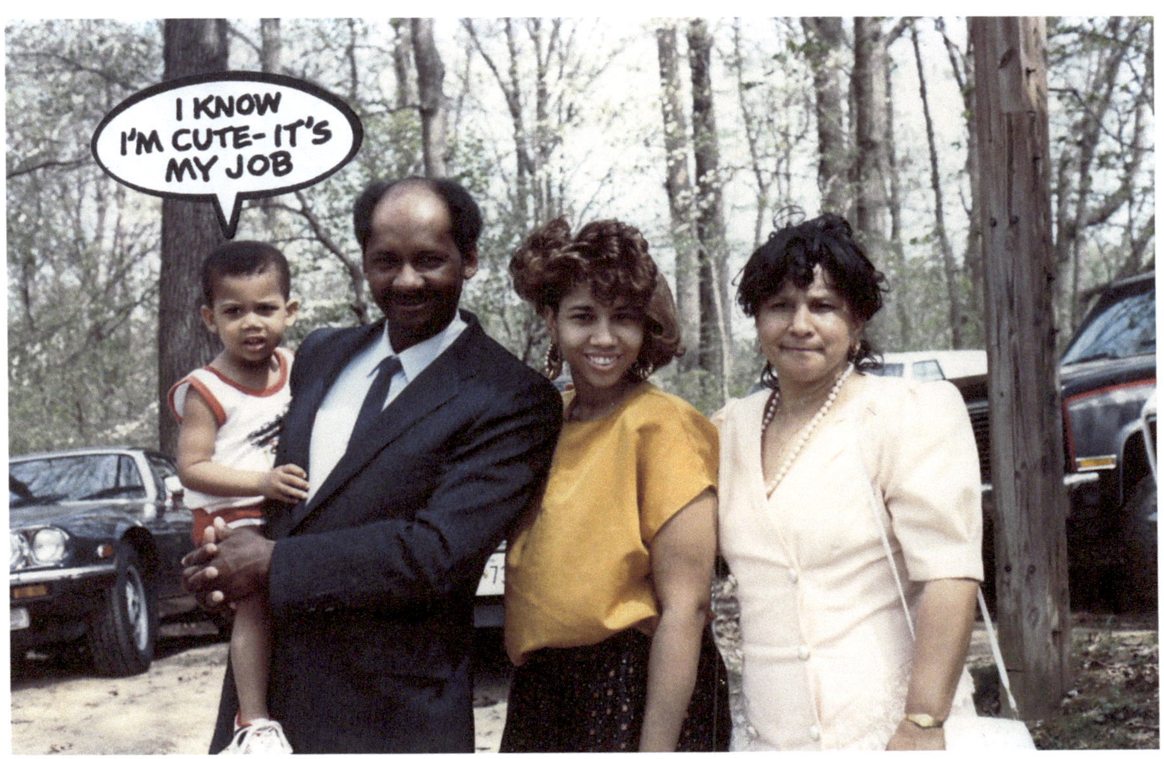
I KNOW
I'M CUTE- IT'S
MY JOB

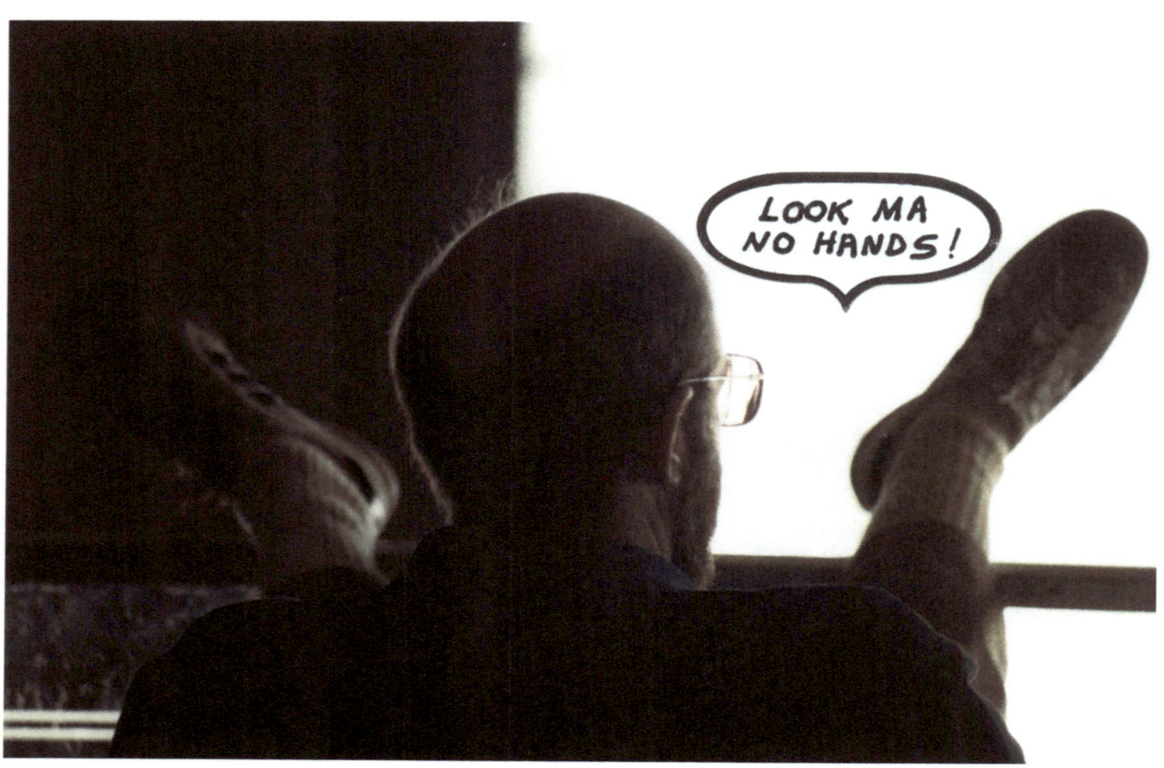
LOOK MA
NO HANDS!

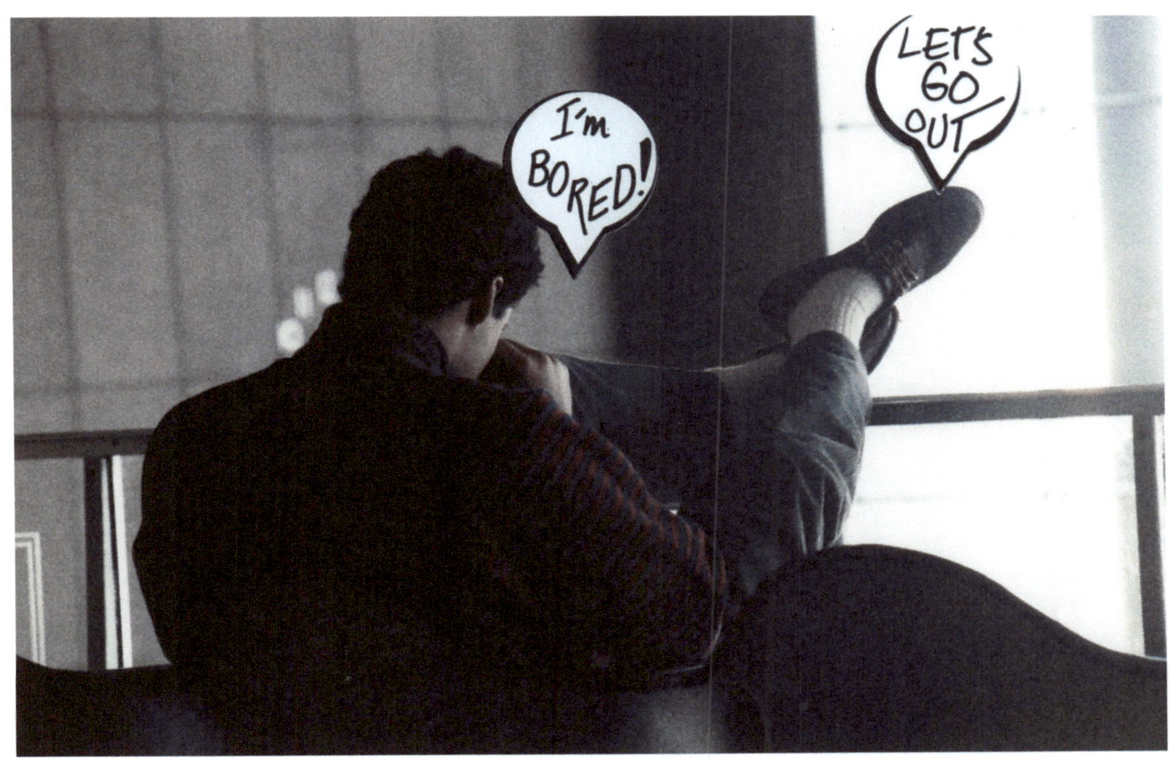
I'm BORED!
LET'S GO OUT

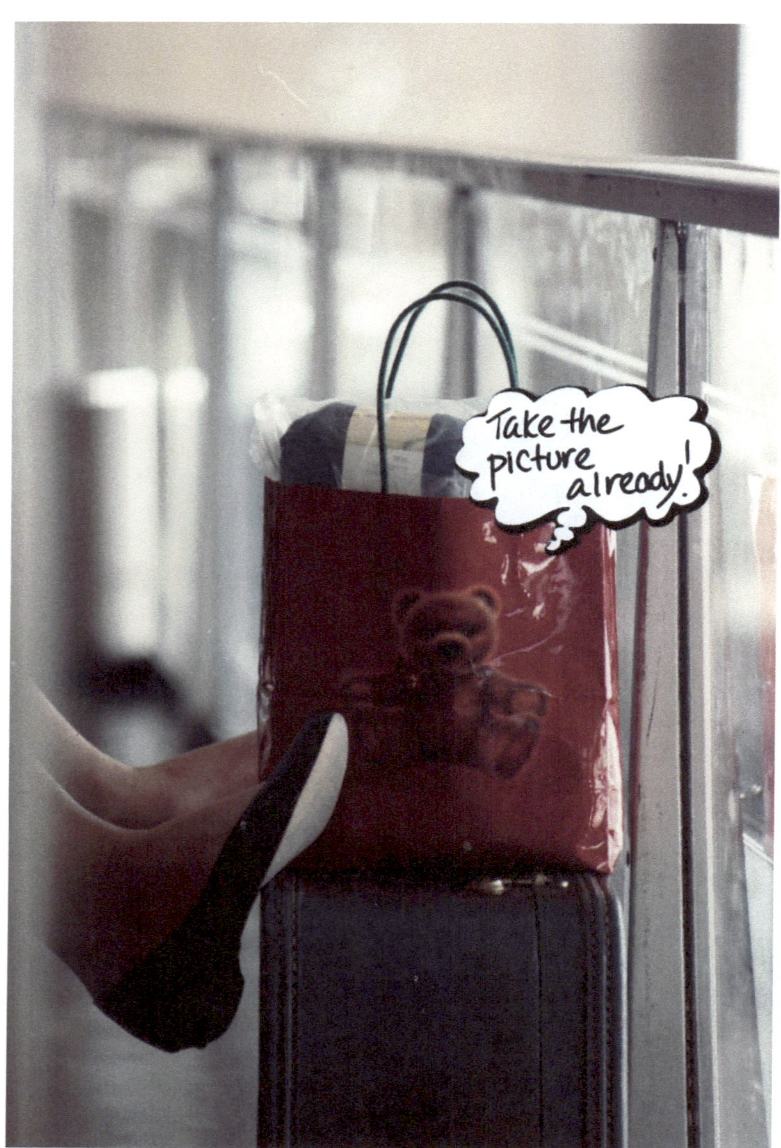
Take the picture already!

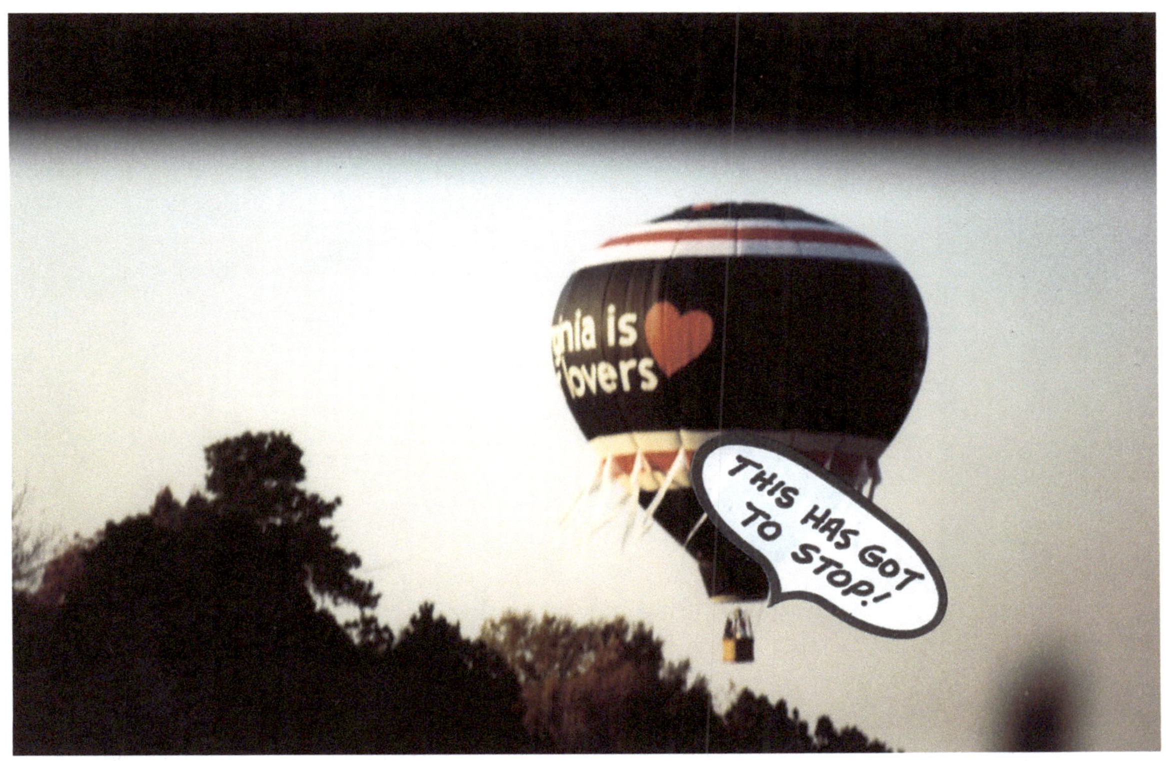
THIS HAS GOT TO STOP!

THIS WON'T HURT A BIT!
PLEASE DEPOSIT COINS

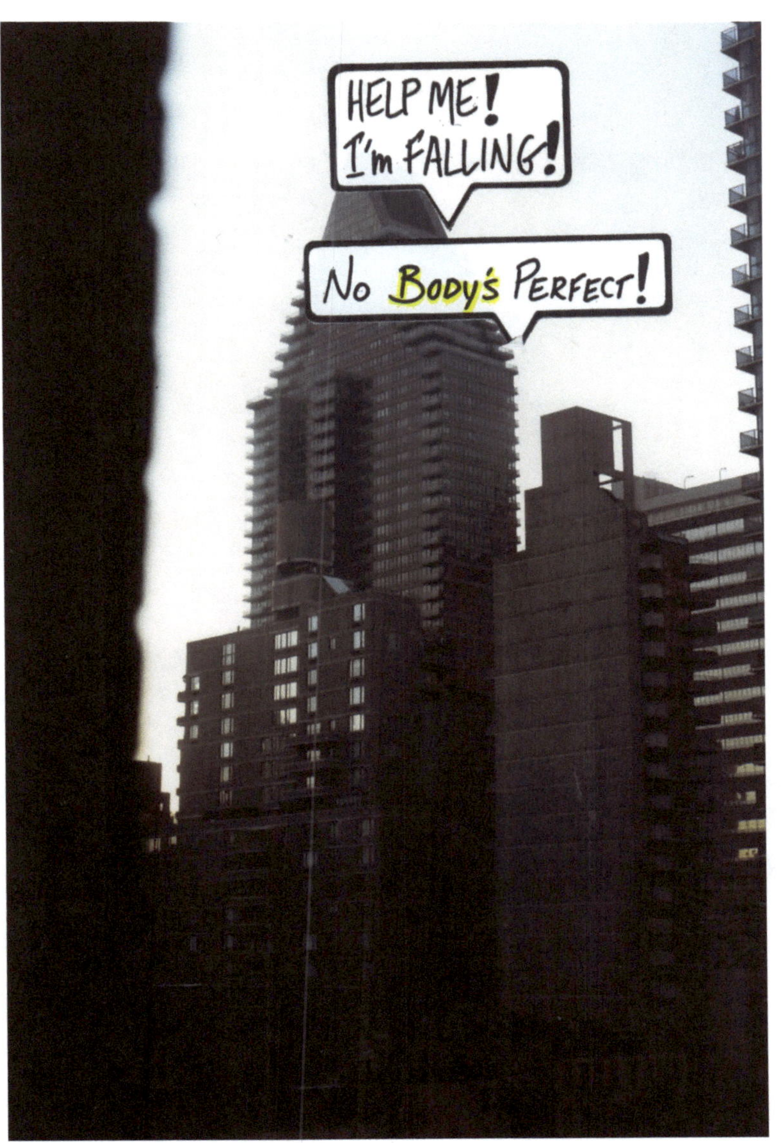
HELP ME!
I'm FALLING!
No BODY'S PERFECT!

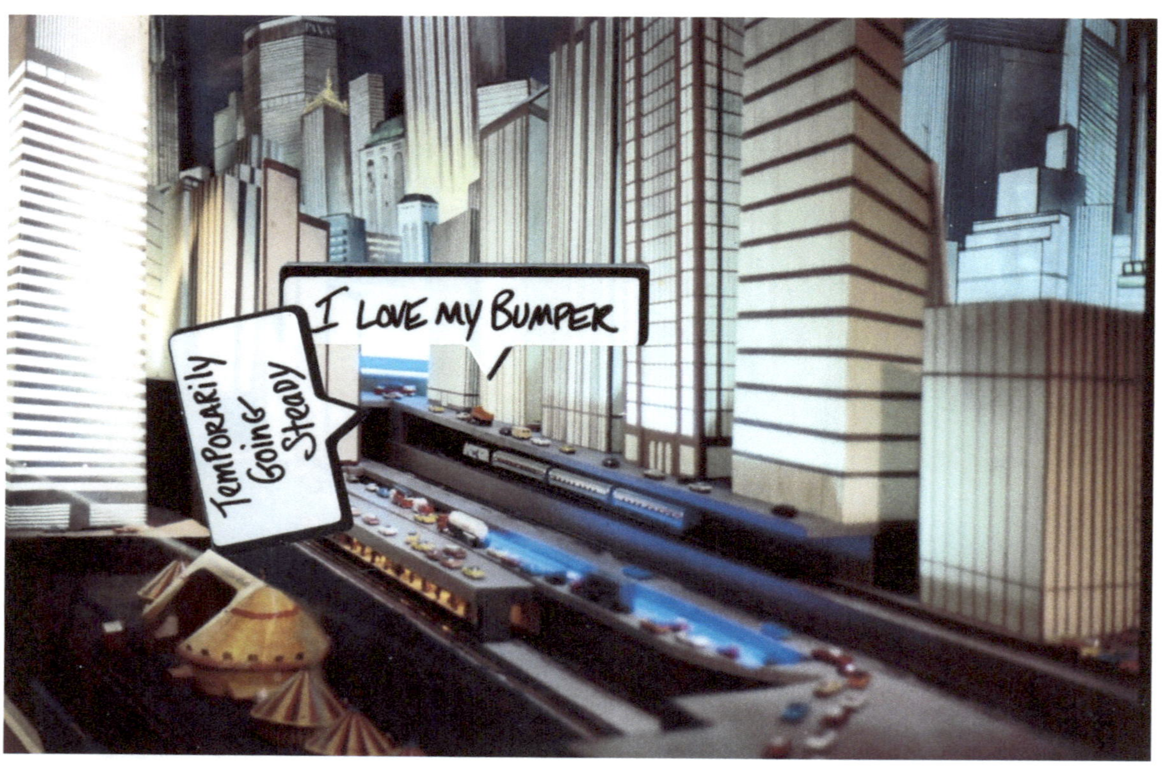
Temporarily Going Steady
I LOVE MY BUMPER

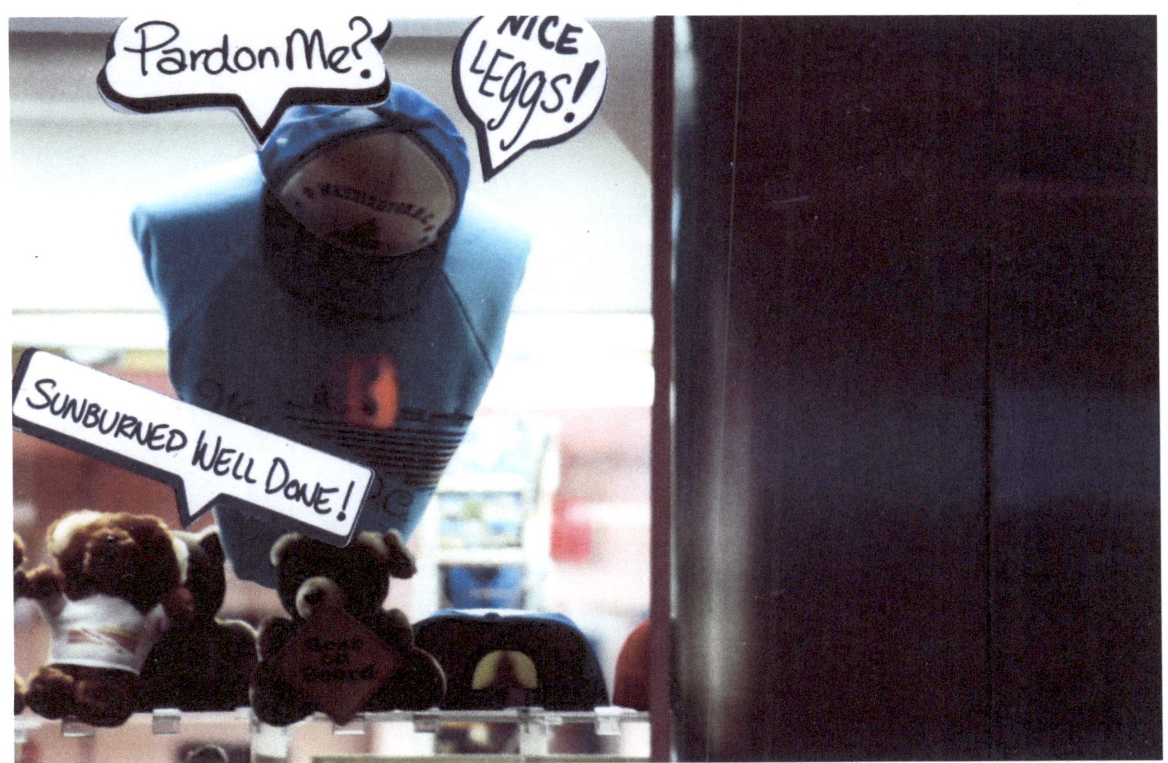
Pardon Me?
NICE LEGGS!
SUNBURNED WELL DONE!

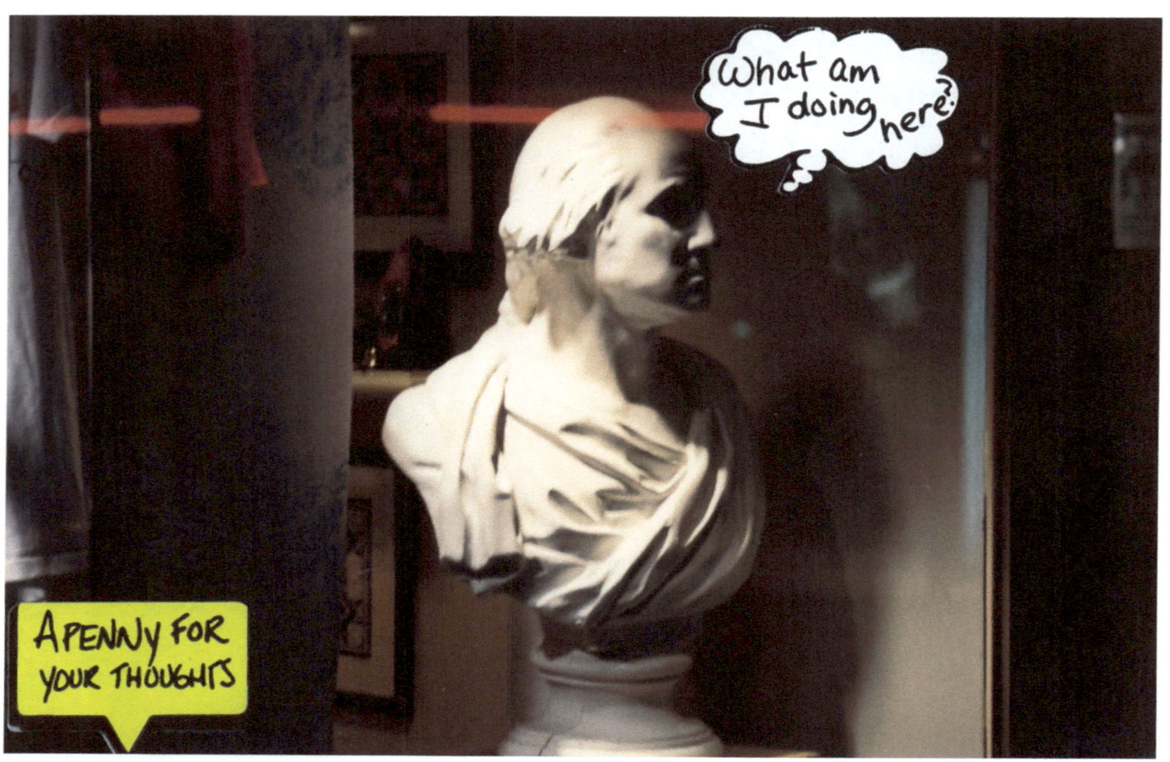
What am I doing here?
A PENNY FOR YOUR THOUGHTS

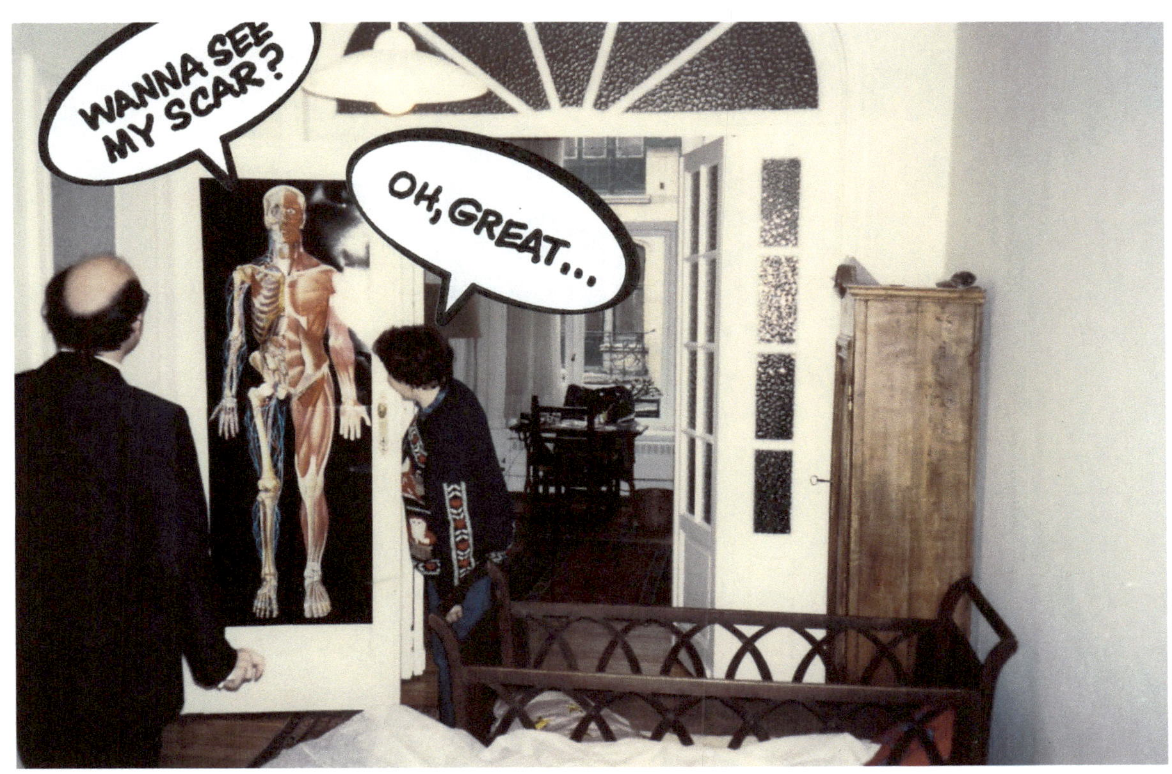
WANNA SEE MY SCAR?
OH, GREAT...

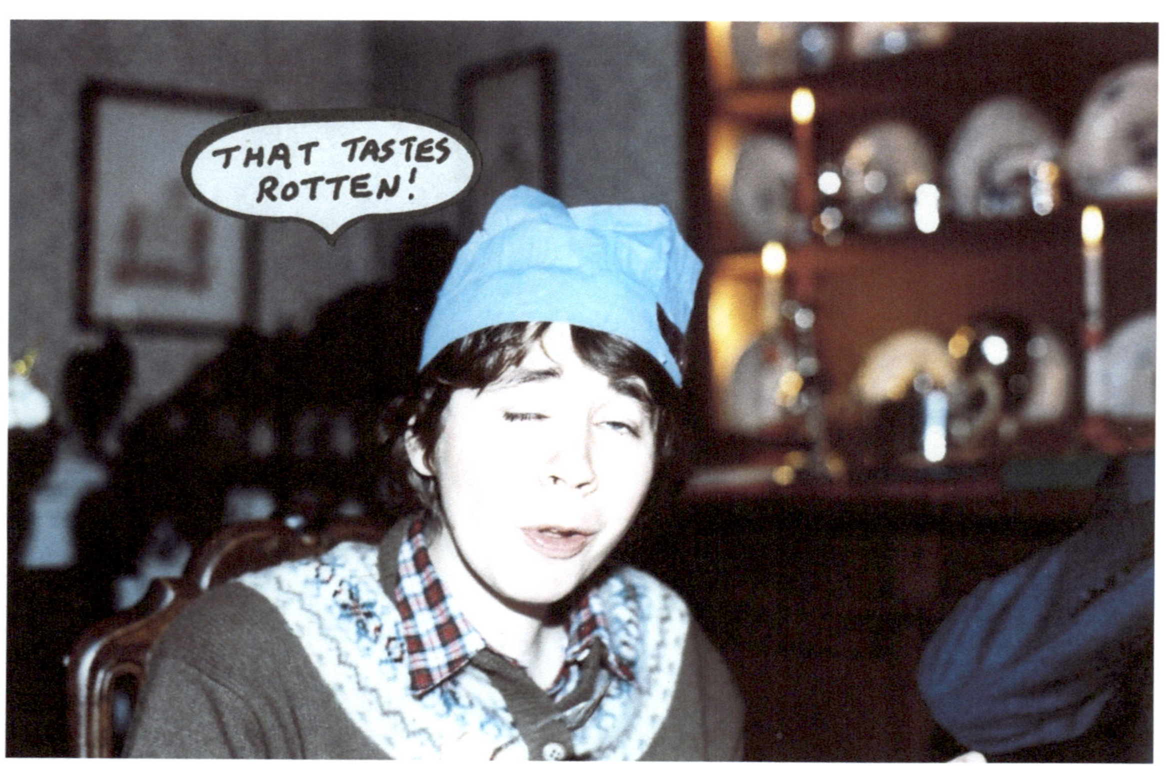
THAT TASTES ROTTEN!

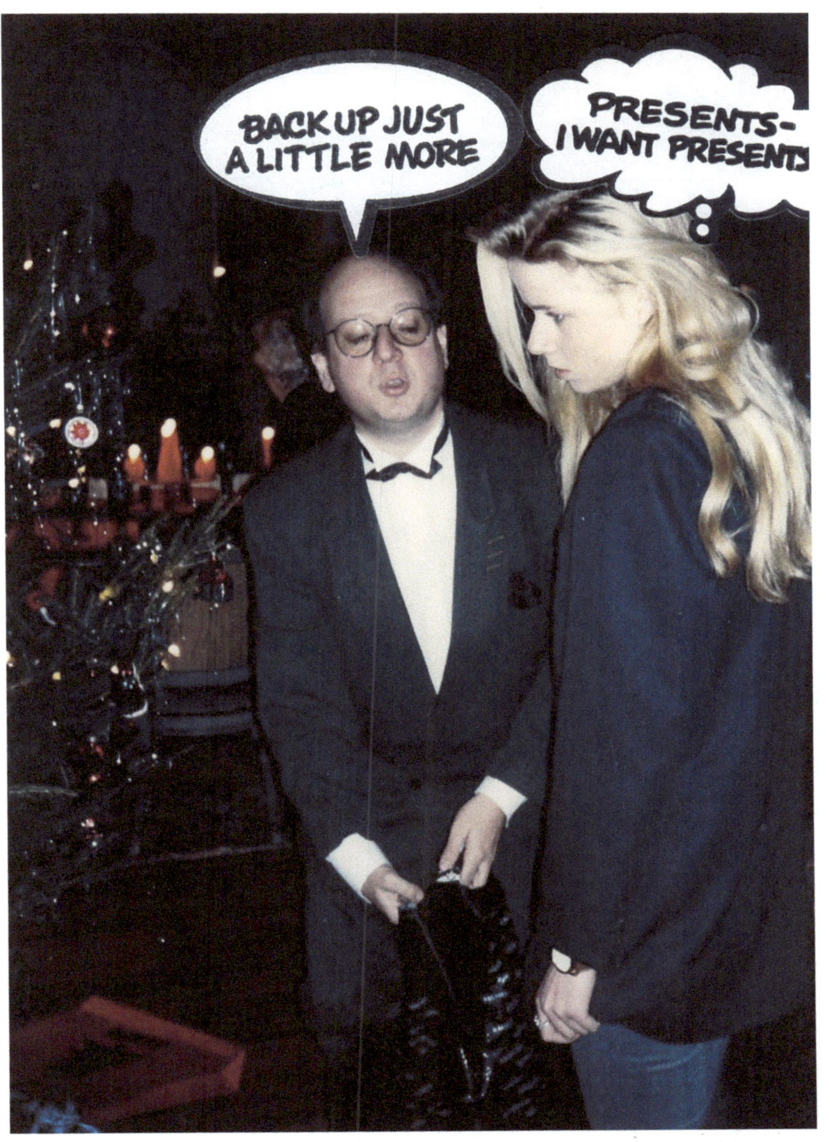
BACK UP JUST
A LITTLE MORE
PRESENTS-
I WANT PRESENTS

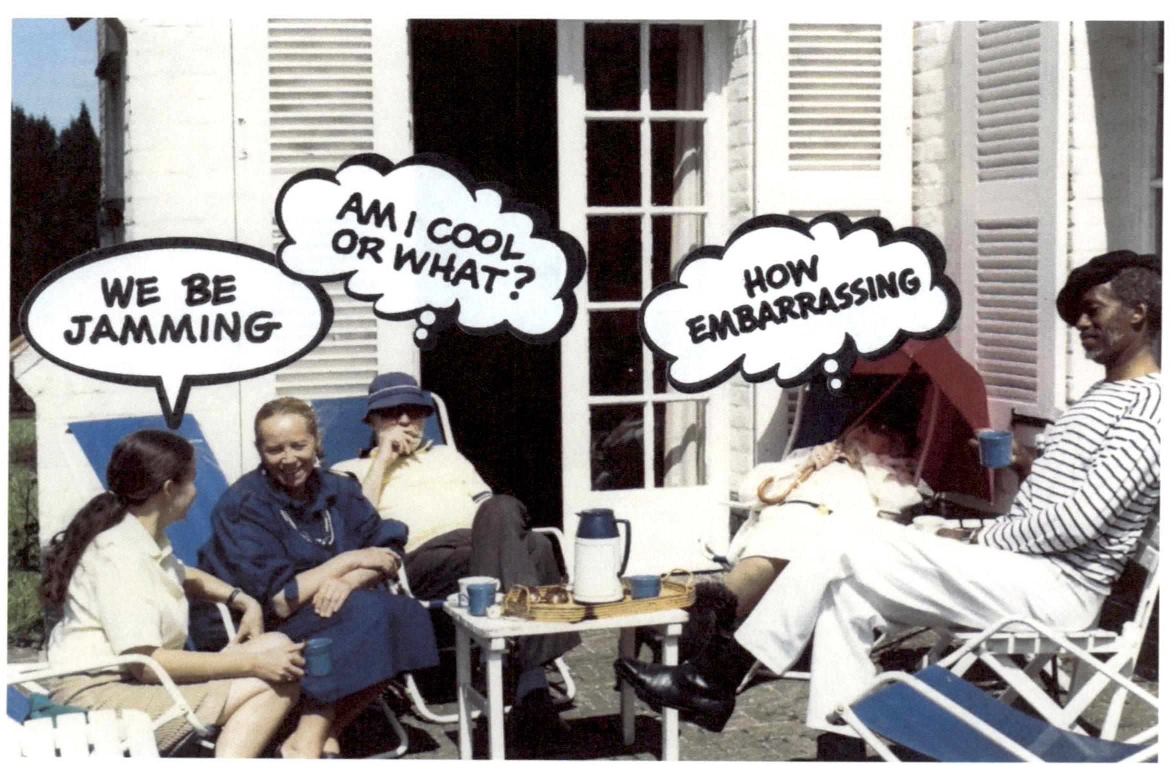
WE BE JAMMING
AM I COOL OR WHAT?
HOW EMBARRASSING

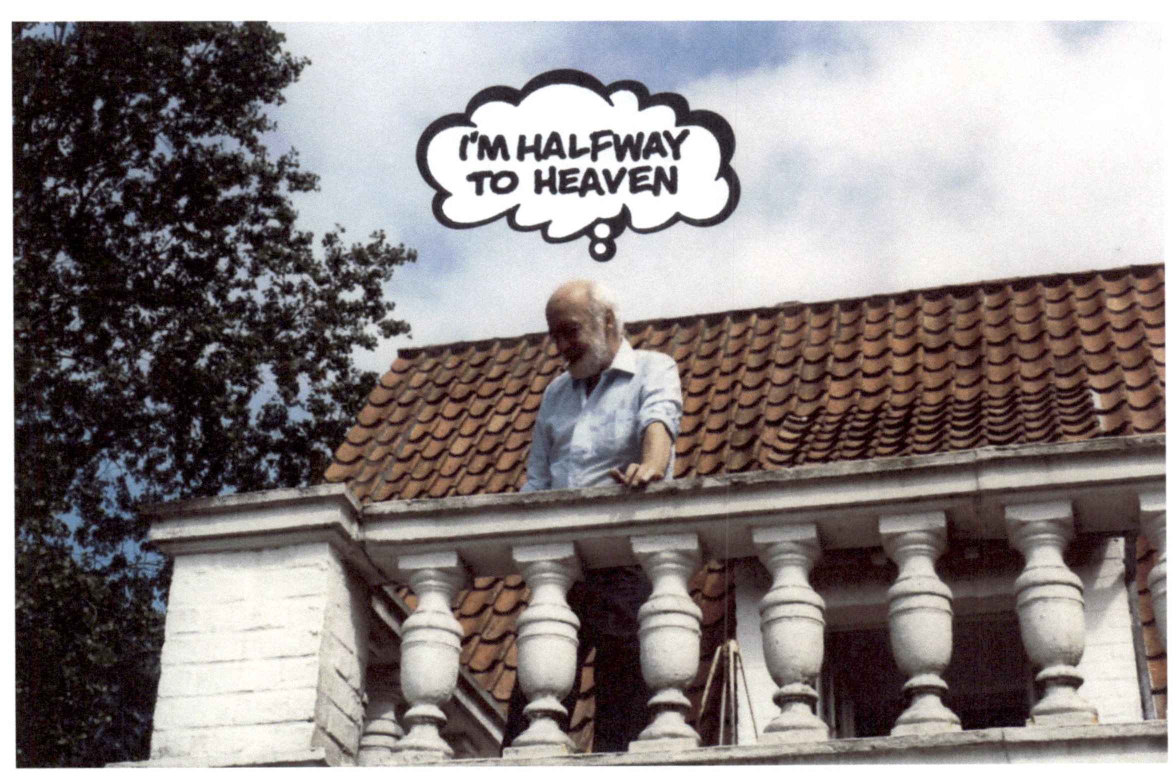
I'M HALFWAY
TO HEAVEN

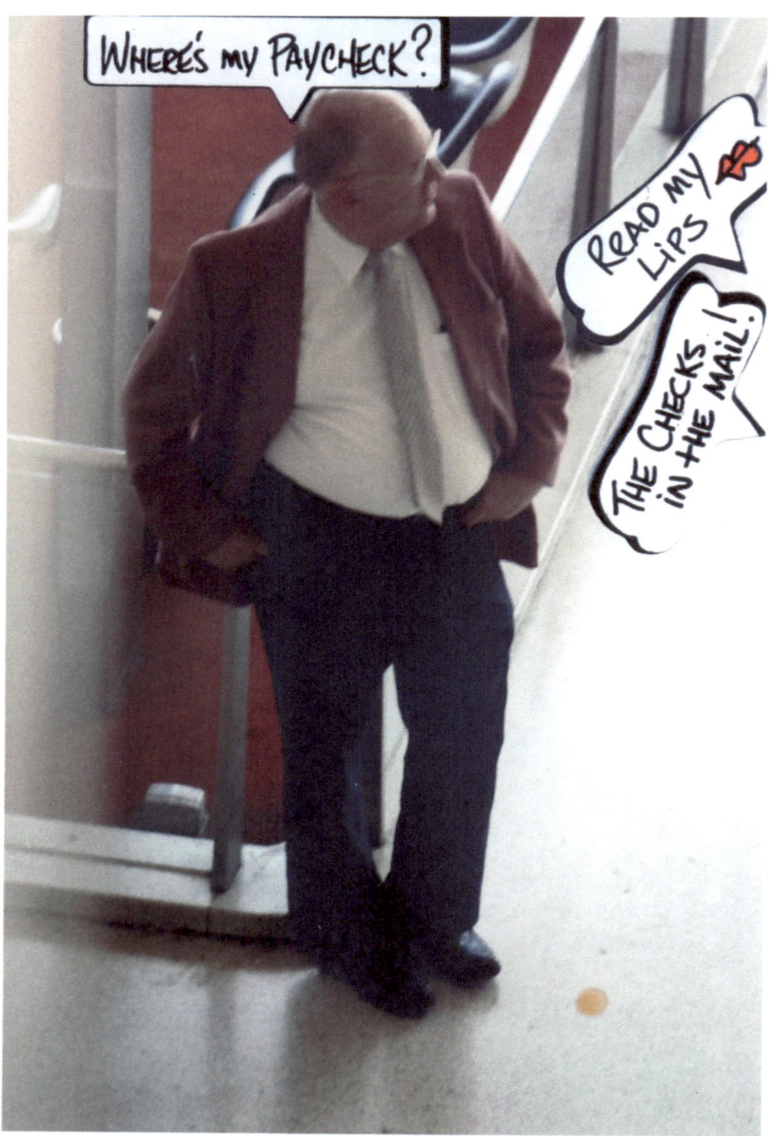
WHERE'S MY PAYCHECK?
READ MY LIPS
THE CHECKS IN THE MAIL!

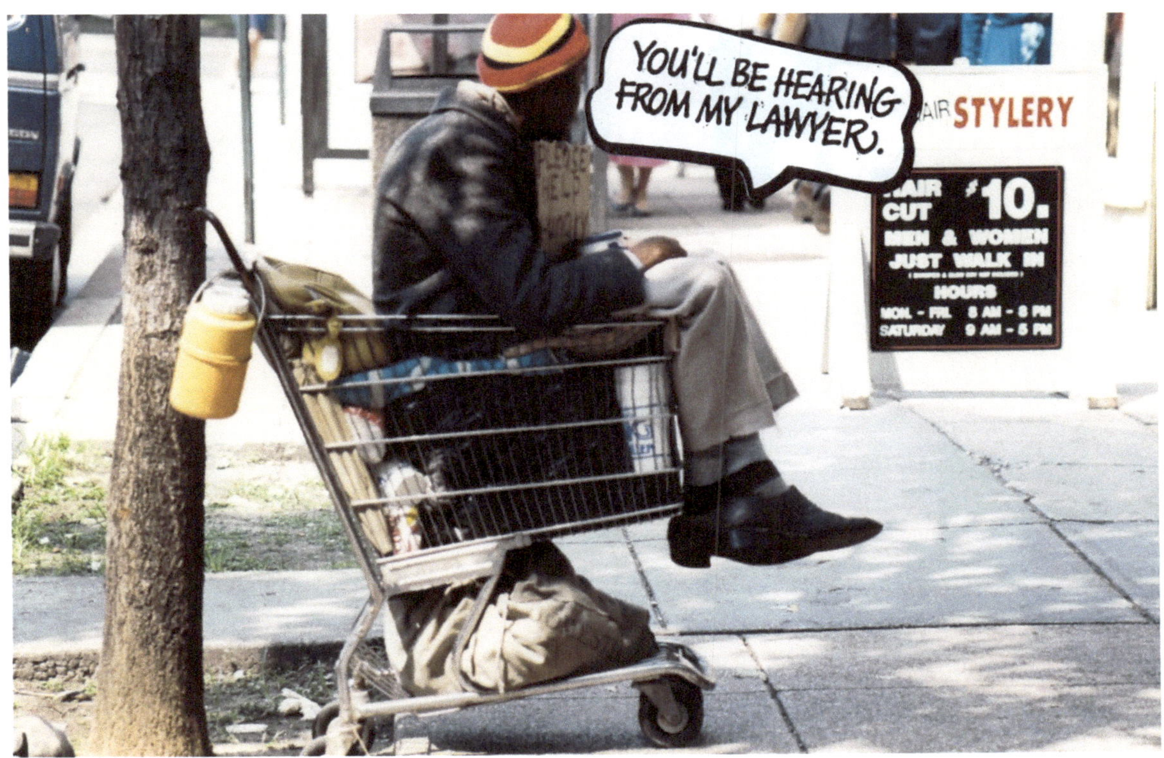
YOU'LL BE HEARING FROM MY LAWYER.
AIR STYLERY
AIR CUT $10.
MEN & WOMEN
JUST WALK IN
HOURS
SATURDAY 9 AM - 5 PM

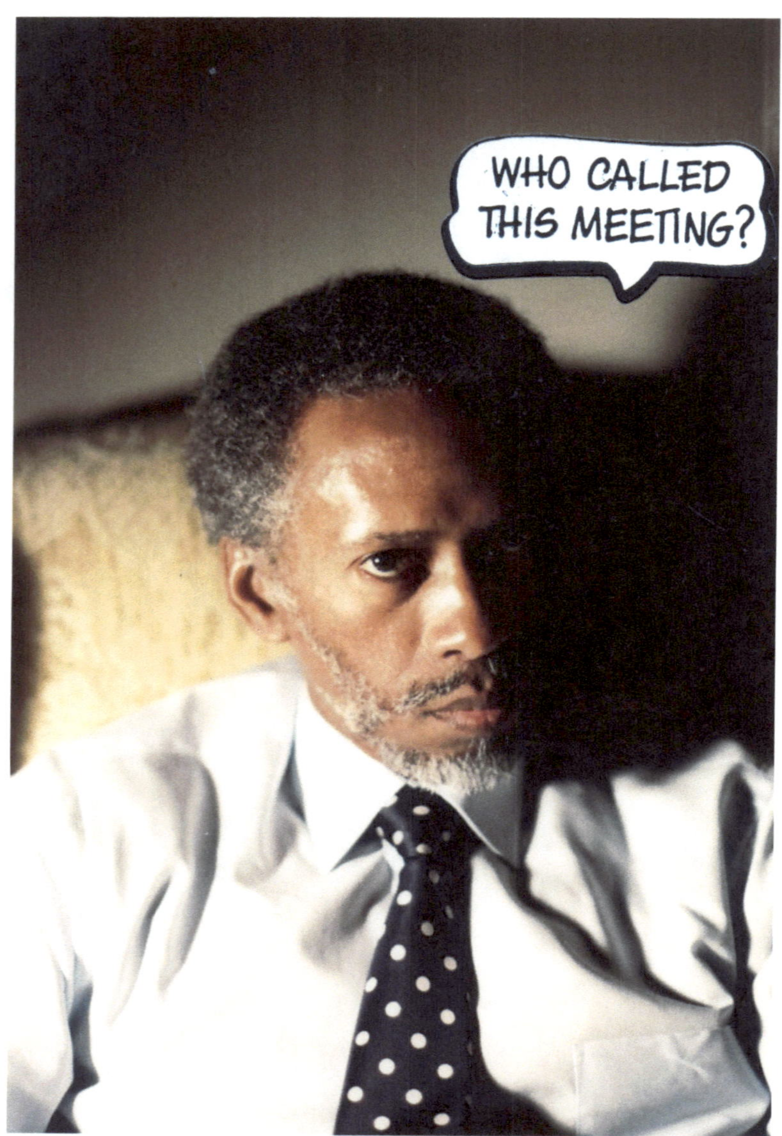
WHO CALLED
THIS MEETING?

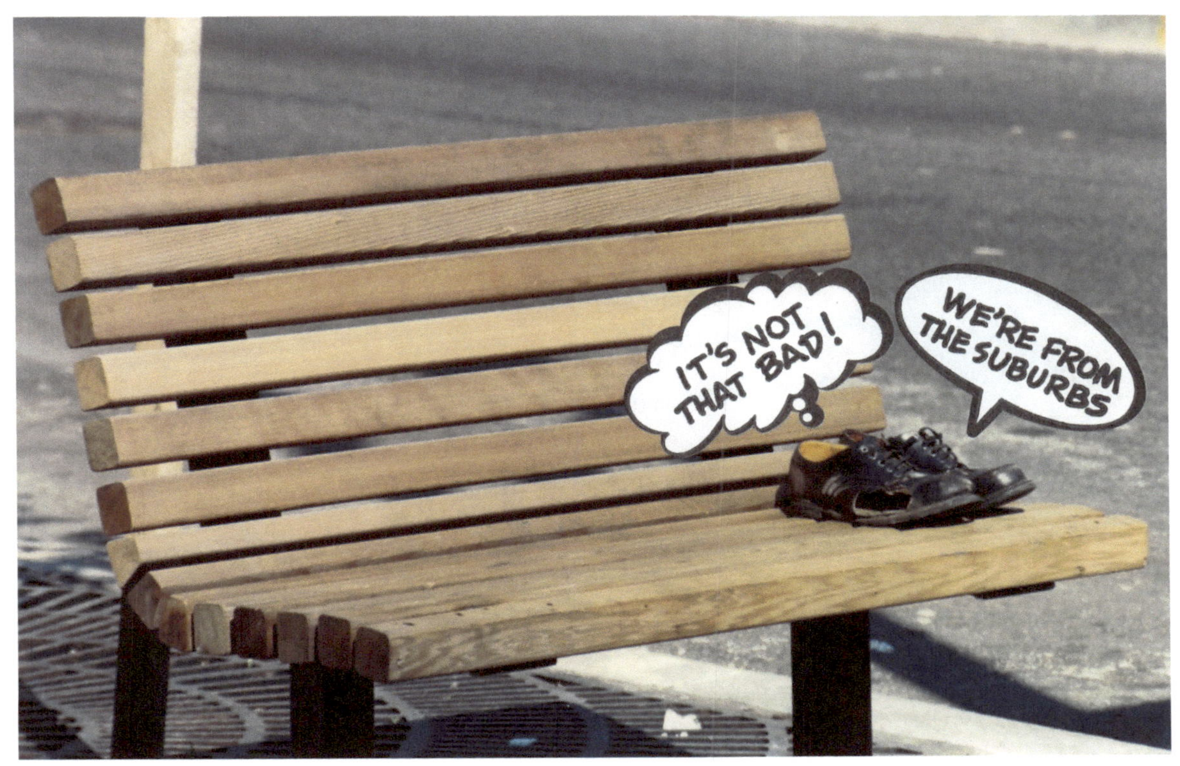
IT'S NOT THAT BAD!
WE'RE FROM THE SUBURBS

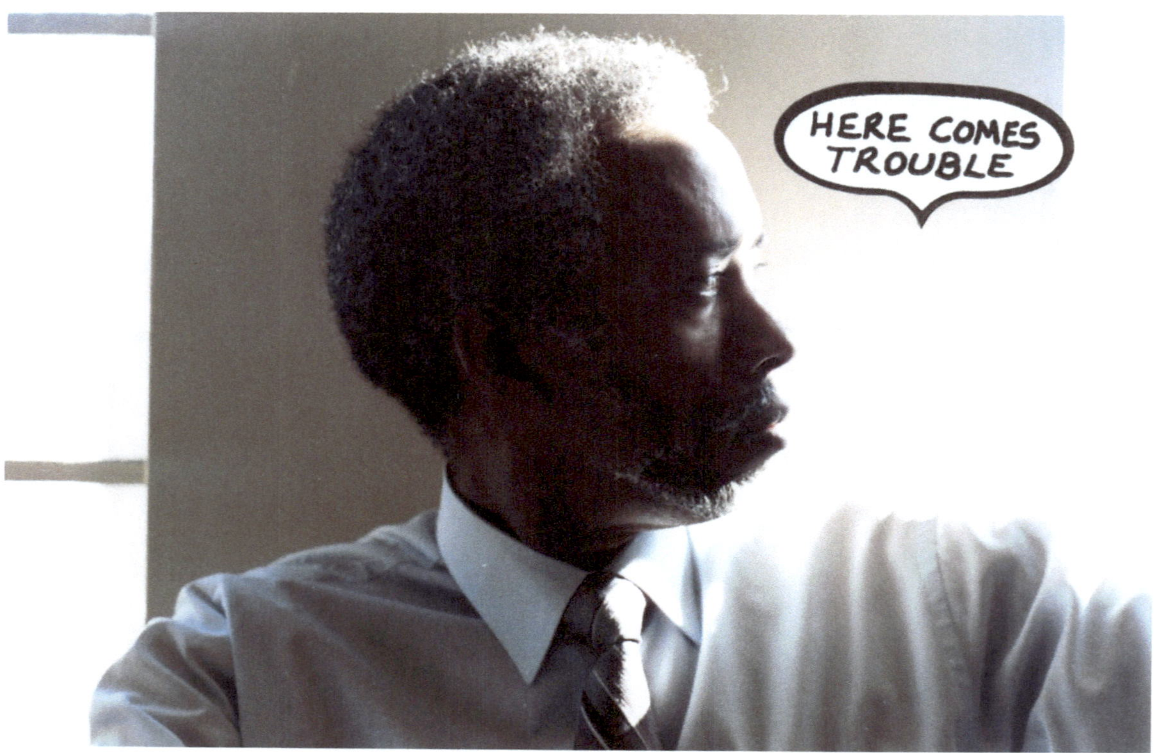
HERE COMES TROUBLE

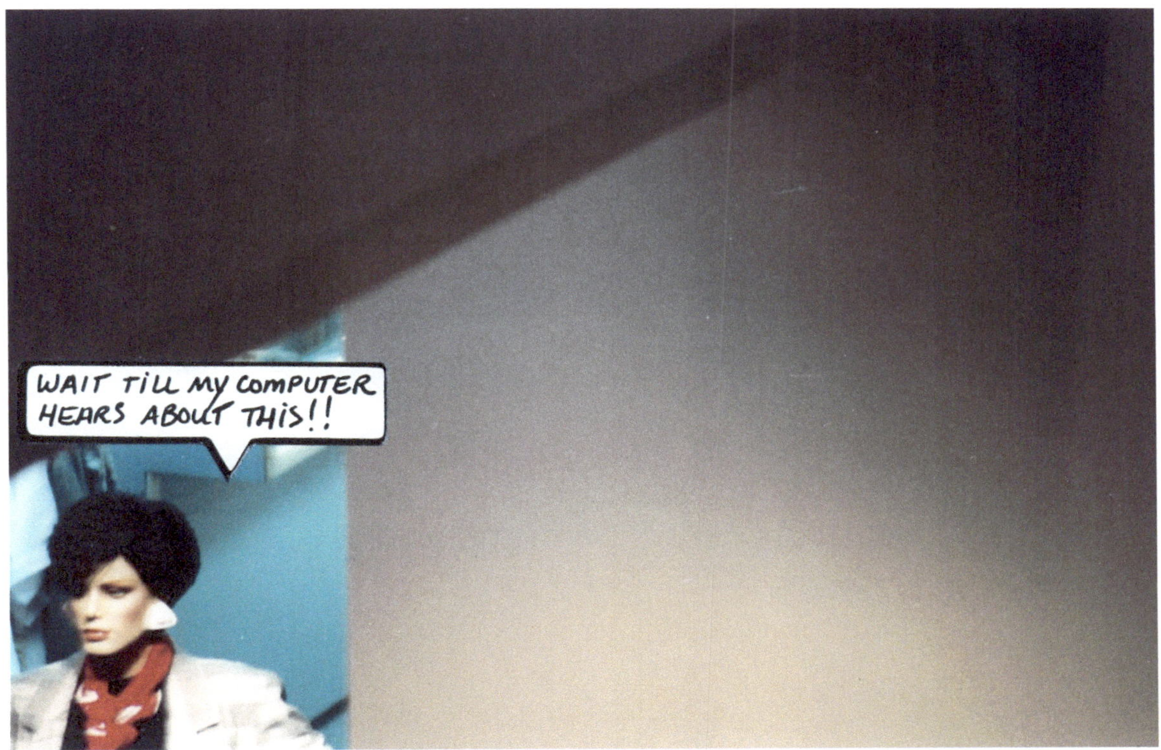
WAIT TILL MY COMPUTER HEARS ABOUT THIS!!

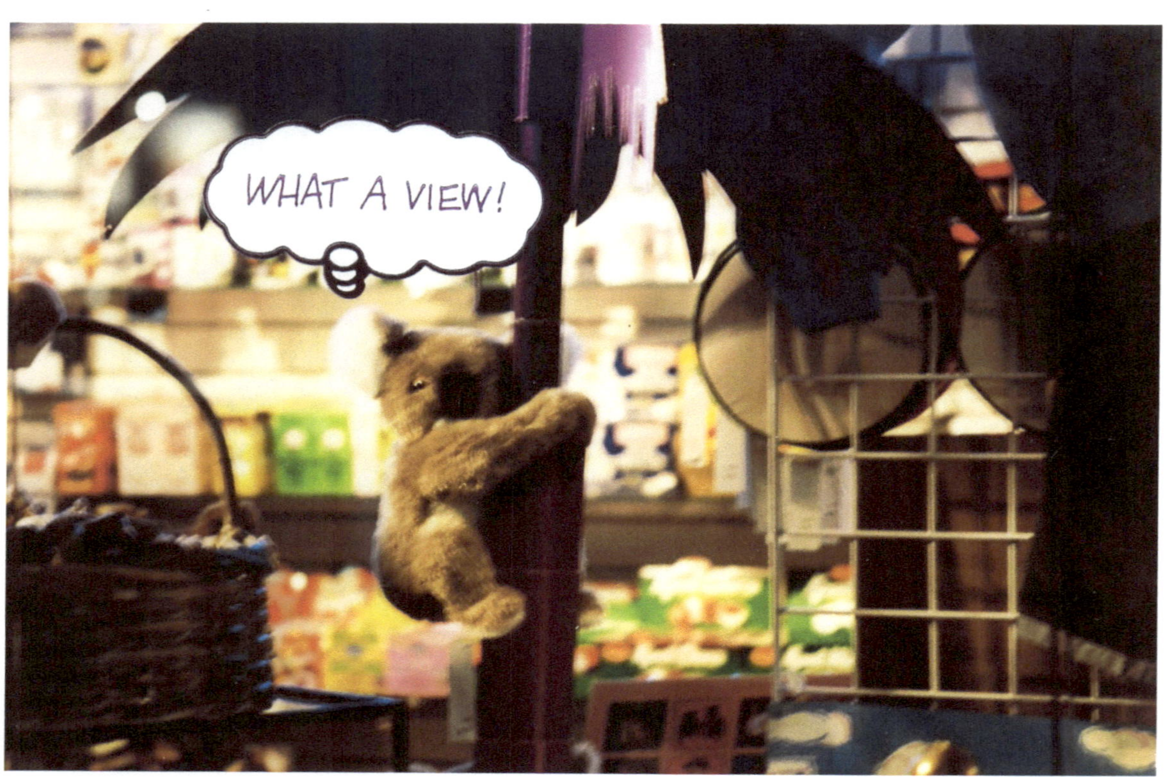
WHAT A VIEW!

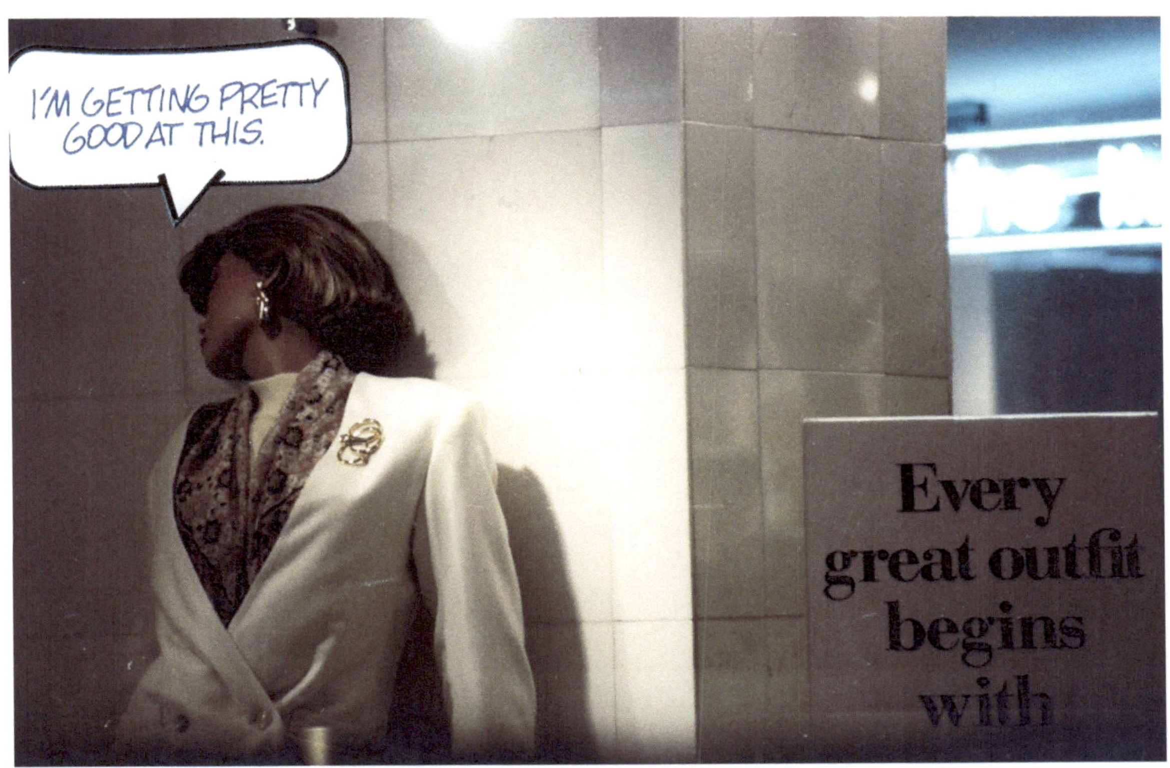
I'M GETTING PRETTY GOOD AT THIS.
Every great outfit begins with

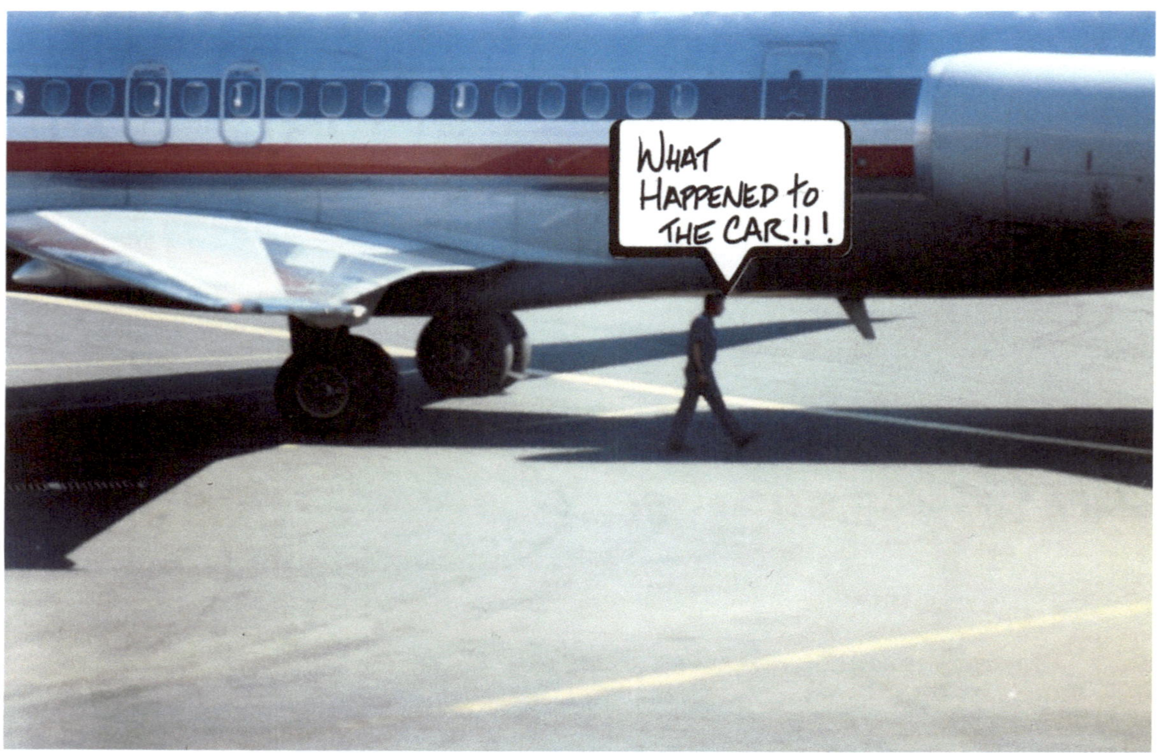
WHAT
HAPPENED to
THE CAR!!!

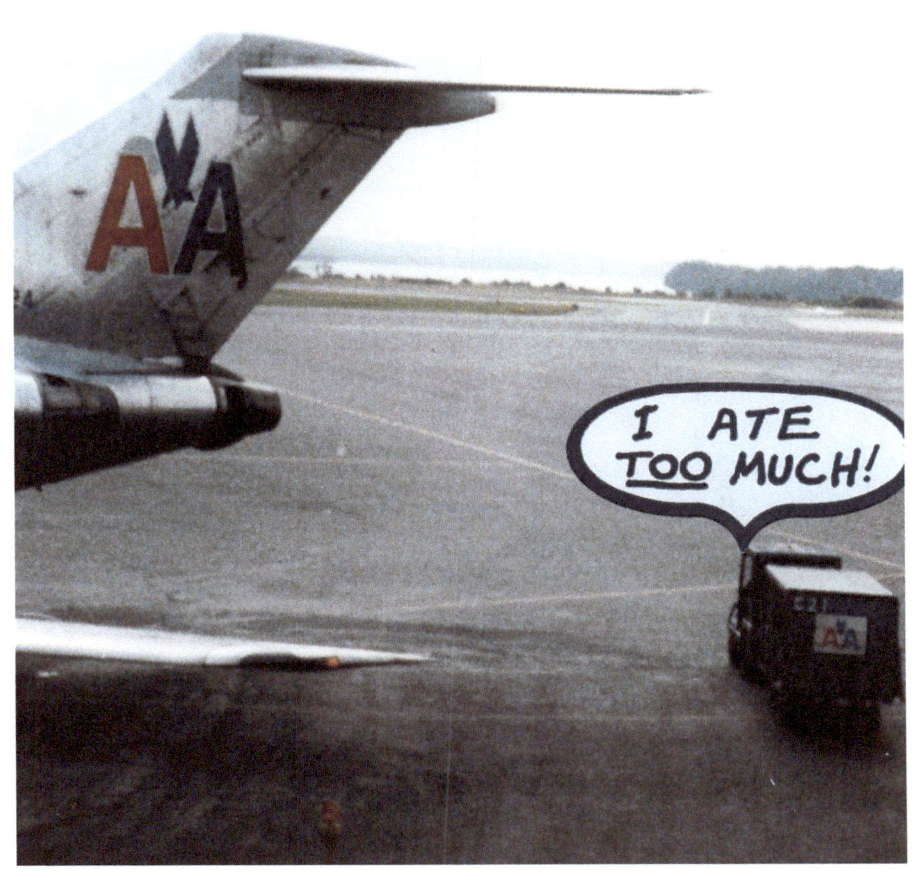
I ATE TOO MUCH!

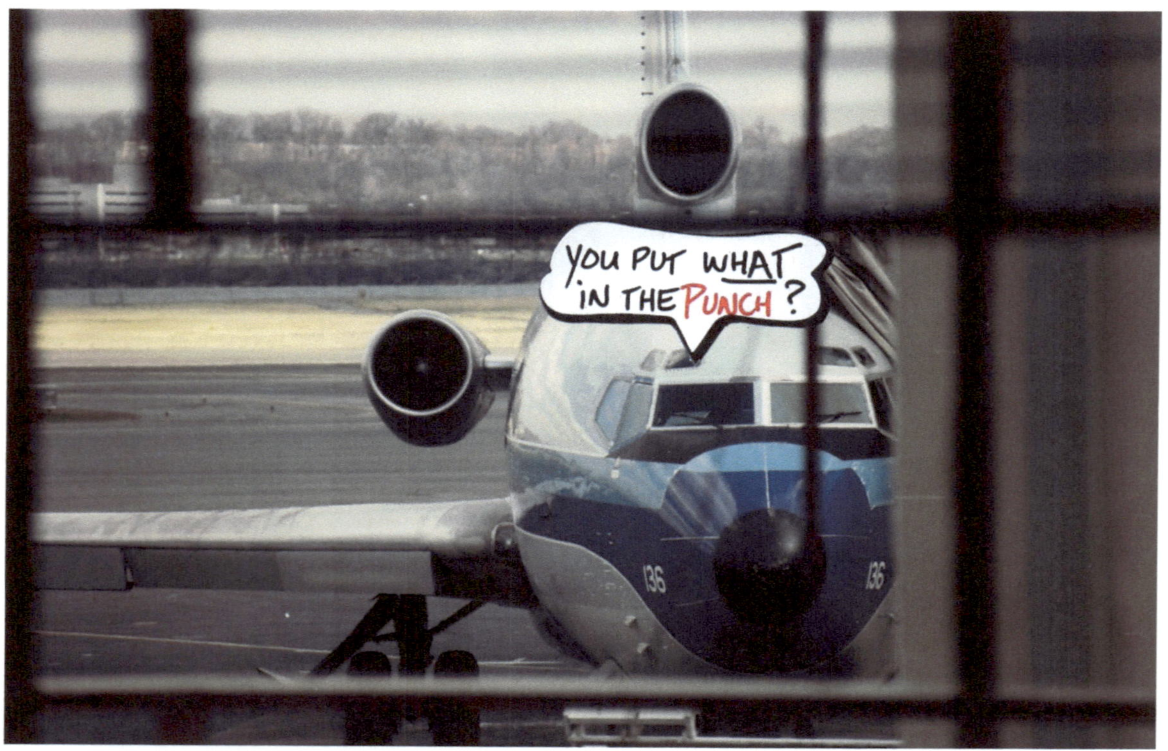
YOU PUT WHAT
IN THE PUNCH?

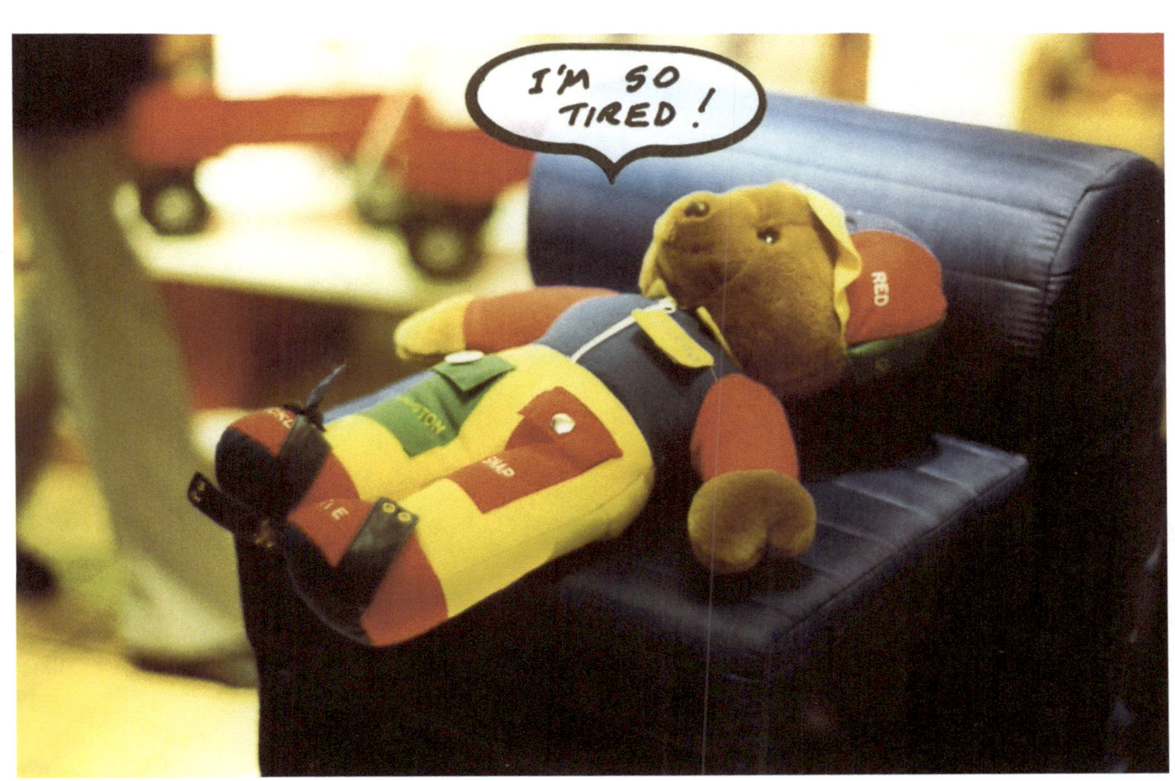
I'M SO TIRED!
RED

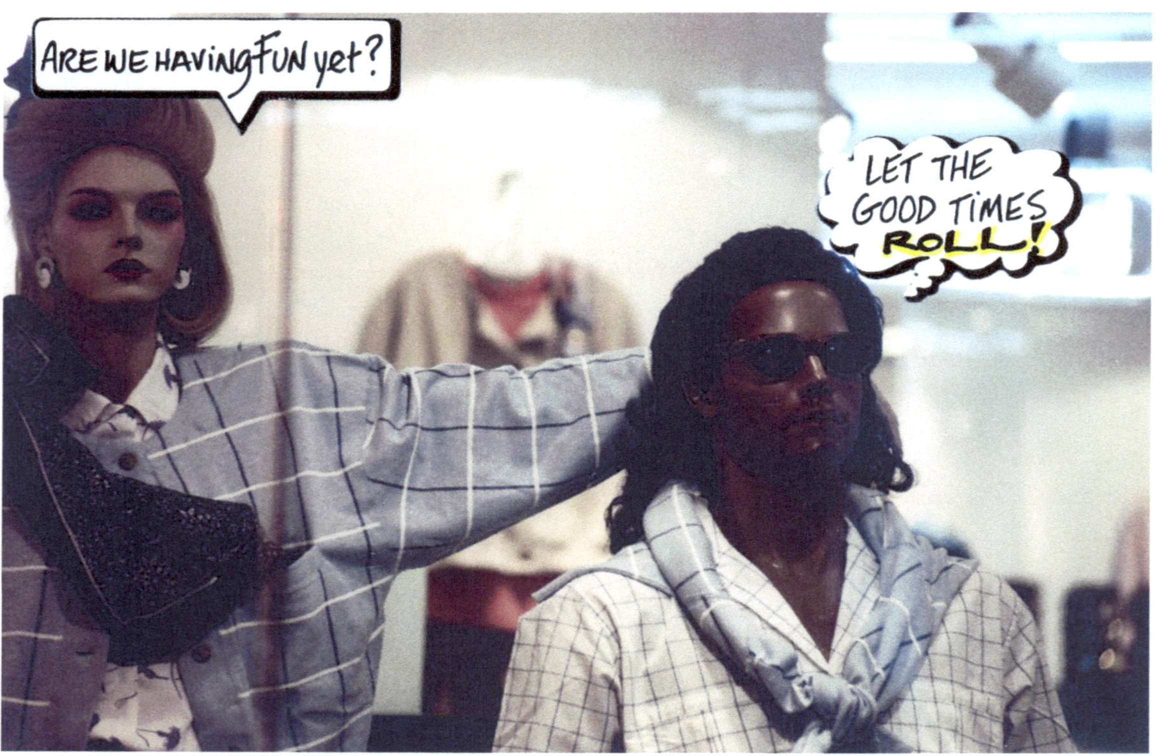
ARE WE HAVING FUN yet?
LET THE GOOD TIMES ROLL!

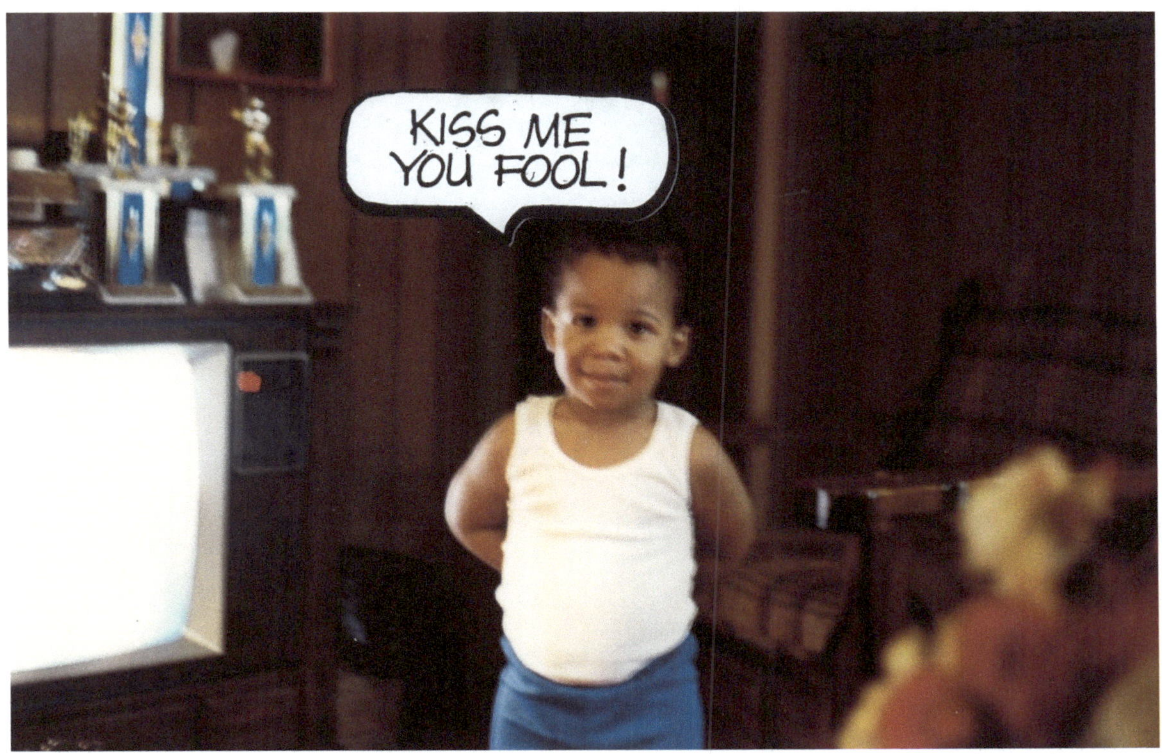
KISS ME
YOU FOOL!

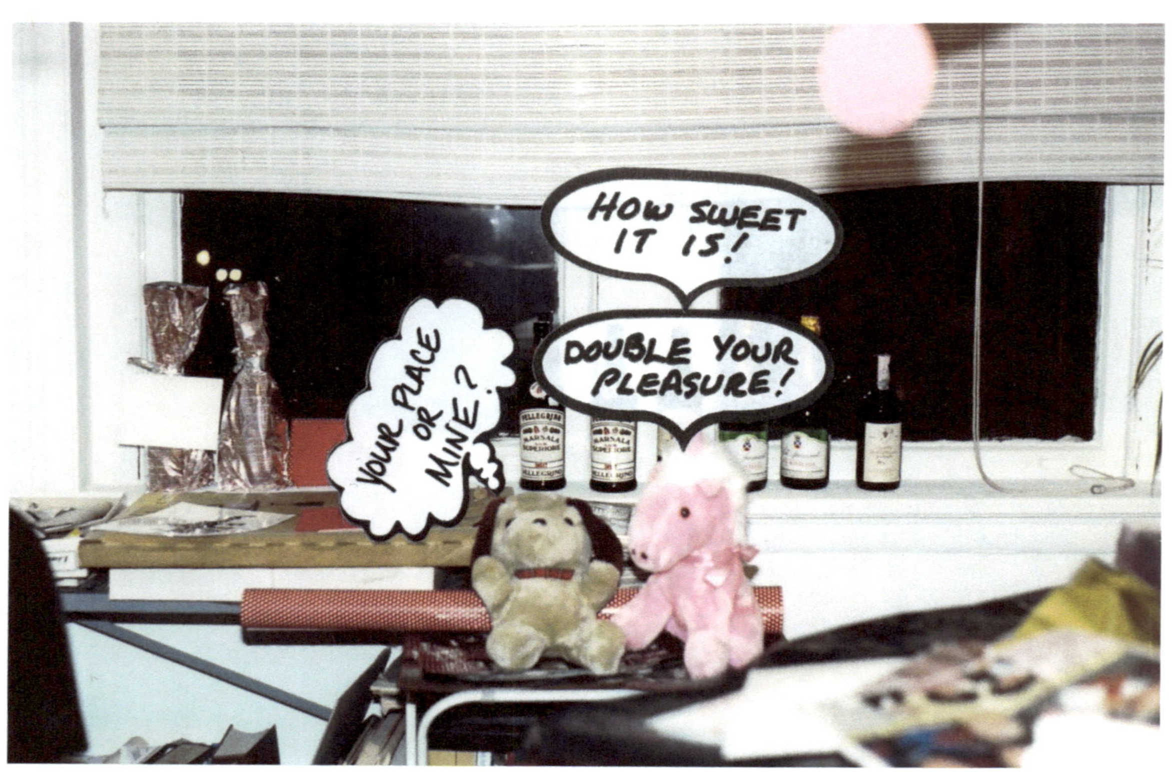
YOUR PLACE OR MINE?
HOW SWEET IT IS!
DOUBLE YOUR PLEASURE!

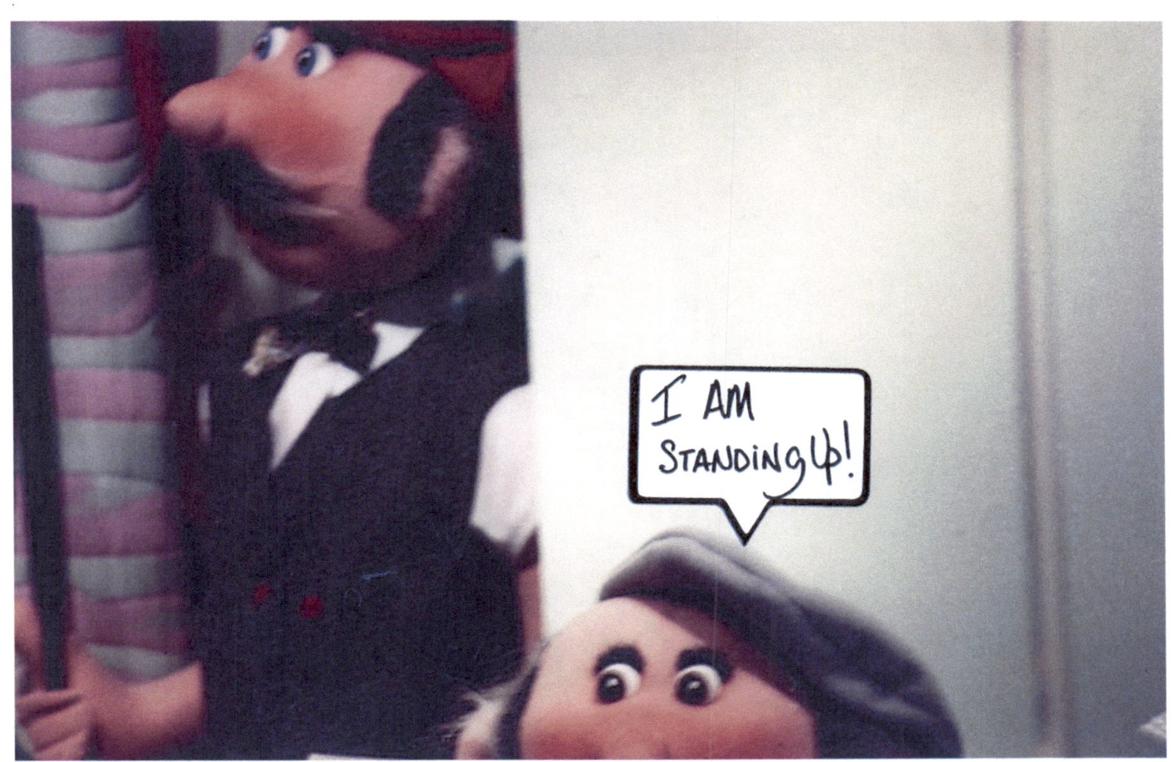
I AM
STANDING UP!

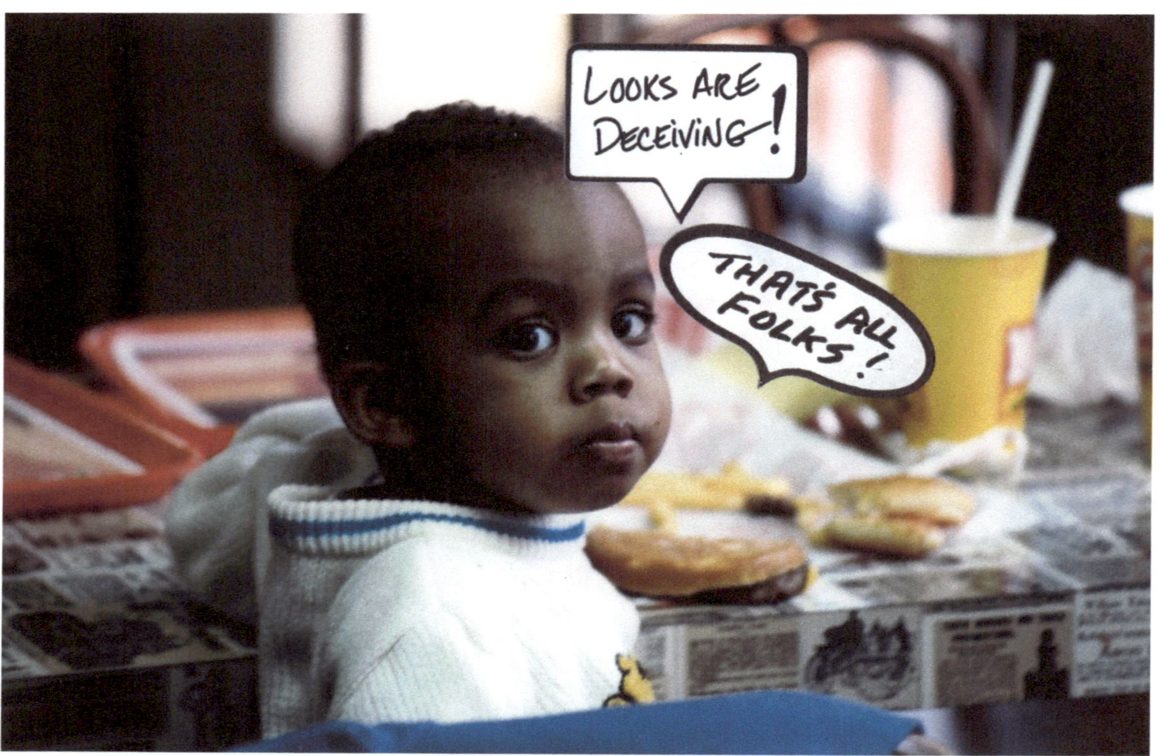
LOOKS ARE DECEIVING!
THAT'S ALL FOLKS!

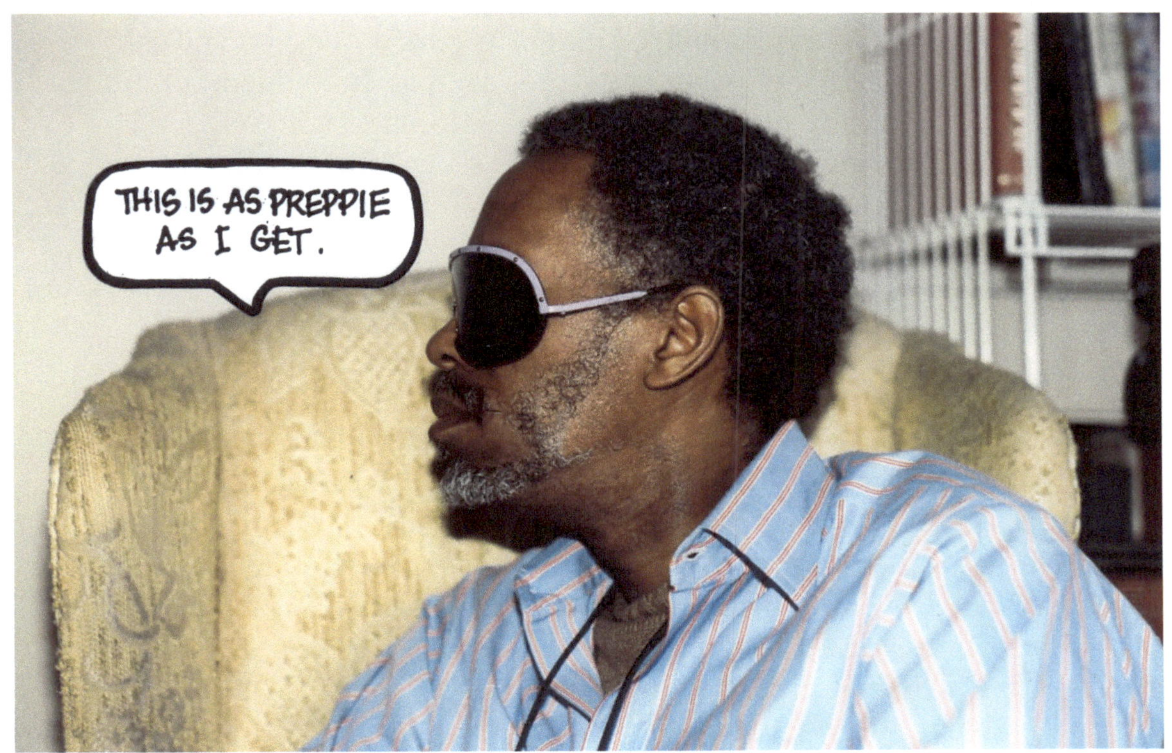
THIS IS AS PREPPIE
AS I GET.

Eugene James Martin (b. Washington, D.C., July 24, 1938 - d. Lafayette, Louisiana, January 1, 2005) was a prolific African American visual artist.

Eugene J. Martin's art is best known for his imaginative, complex mixed media collages on paper, his often gently humorous pencil and pen and ink drawings, and his paintings on paper and canvas that may incorporate whimsical allusions to animal, machine and structural imagery among areas of "pure", constructed, biomorphic, or disciplined lyrical abstraction.

Eugene Martin's works of art can be found in numerous private art collections throughout the world, and are included in the permanent collection of the Ogden Museum of Southern Art, New Orleans; the Alexandria Museum of Art, Louisiana; the Stowitts Museum & Library in Pacific Grove, California; the Munich Museum of Modern Art; the Arthur Schomburg Center for Research in Black Culture, New York; the Mobile Museum of Art, Alabama; the Walter O. Evans Collection of African American Art in Savannah, Georgia, the Paul R. Jones Collection of African American Art at the University of Delaware, the Walter Anderson Museum of Art in Ocean Springs, Mississippi, and the Louisiana State University Museum of Art in the Shaw Center for the Arts in Baton Rouge, Louisiana.

http://www.artnet.com/awc/eugene-j-martin.html

http://www.artstor.org/what-is-artstor/w-html/col-martin.shtml

http://www.youtube.com/nemastoma

www.ingramcontent.com/pod-product-compliance
Lightning Source LLC
LaVergne TN
LVHW070143110826
845147LV00002B/313

9780578030432